CLASSICAL WEDGWOOD DESIGNS

Endymion on Latmos. *Wedgwood plaque*. (See page 52.)

CLASSICAL
WEDGWOOD
DESIGNS

Carol Macht, A.M., Ph.D.

THE SOURCES AND THEIR USE AND THE RELATIONSHIP
OF WEDGWOOD JASPER WARE TO THE CLASSICAL
REVIVAL OF THE EIGHTEENTH CENTURY

1957

M. BARROWS AND COMPANY

NEW YORK

To Dr. David I. Macht, my father-in-law,
who taught me the humility and the satisfaction of scholarship

ACKNOWLEDGMENTS

I wish to express my deep obligation to Professor David Moore Robinson, who suggested the subject and whose unflagging interest in the research necessary for this book and many helpful suggestions have made it possible. I should like to thank Dr. Charles Gauss for reading the manuscript, Miss Annarie Peters for typing and editing, and Dr. Sarah Freeman for the photographs. Josiah Wedgwood & Sons supplied additional photographic material which is gratefully acknowledged.

Contents

Preface

———

THE EIGHTEENTH CENTURY CERTAINLY LOOKED AT ITSELF in a classical mirror. It was a three-panelled mirror, however, and sometimes the images overlapped to make a new composite, the particular and individual portrait of the Classic Revival. One panel was western man's classical birthright of speech, law, social custom, a heritage he couldn't renounce in even his most gothic moods. And the eighteenth century was so far from medieval in temper that it not only cleared away as much of the middle ages as it could afford to, it spelled out its disdain in the word "gothick" itself.

Another panel of the eighteenth-century mirror was its serene conviction that classical letters contained all the law and prophets. As Edward Gibbon put it, "the principal benefits of a familiar intercourse with Greece and Rome" consisted among other things of "the temperate dignity of style, the graceful proportions of art, the forms of visible and intellectual beauty, the just delineation of character and passion, the rhetoric of narrative and argument, the regular fabric of epic and dramatic poetry."

The third panel was the eighteenth century's own invention of classical archaeology. This "romantic phenomenon" happened with characteristic system and thoroughness in one remarkable five-year period. Herculaneum was first described in a letter published by Winkelmann in 1762 and in 1767 his "Monumenti Antichi Inediti" came out. James Stuart, "Athenian" Stuart as his contemporaries nicknamed him, began to publish the "Antiquities of Athens" in 1762 and Robert Adam reported the "Ruins of the Palace of Diocletian" in 1764.

It isn't surprising that Josiah Wedgwood should be one of the first figures to step out of such a looking-glass. Few people were as influential on the taste, the whole outward look of the time and probably no one, not even Gibbon, so fully personified the Classic Revival in eighteenth-century England. But it is a most pleasant surprise to find him set forth with the combination of wit and skill these pages show. And the combination is altogether in the spirit of the eighteenth century which took its classical studies seriously but also believed in leavening scholarship with grace.

Philip R. Adams

Director of Cincinnati Art Museum
Cincinnati, Ohio

Backgrounds

MUCH HAS BEEN WRITTEN REGARDING THE LIFE AND WORK of Josiah Wedgwood, so much that, had he led a less exemplary life, it would be somewhat embarrassing to his numerous living descendants. This book, however, is not particularly concerned either with the personal life of the potter or with the technical problems of ceramic production. It attempts to show how Wedgwood ware, in its source of design, its manner of conception, and its tremendous popular appeal exemplified, and, indeed, became a characteristic symbol of, the taste of its times.

The eighteenth century, in which the Wedgwood factory was founded, was the great period of the Classic Revival, an amazing romantic phenomenon.[1] It was a period in which the "antique" became a mania. Great collections were passionately begun; academies in Rome, which already had been established in the previous century, flourished with renewed vigor; antiquarian societies were founded; and the enthusiasm for any and all things ancient (meaning, of course, things Greek and Roman) waxed so great that the profitable business of forgery became rampant. We even find Natter, a famous gem engraver of the eighteenth century, saying in defense of his trade, ". . . But he that sells a modern copy of an antique for an original, not he that makes it, is to be blamed." [2]

The only objects other than forgeries which could satisfy the colossal demand for *les choses antiques* were good copies honestly made and sold as such. First, these were in exact imitation of the original; then, in various other materials that served to bring out the design—for example, plaster for statues, reliefs, and urns; painted plaques for wall paintings; painted earthenware for highly glazed vases; glass paste, sulphur, and, finally, pottery for gems. There was assembled a huge fund of classical designs from which single motifs or parts of motifs were taken. Divorced from their original contexts (sarcophagus, urn, altar, wall painting, gem, coin, etc.) the individual motifs, figures, and shapes were used at will. Thus, in a single composition the artist may have utilized a figure from a gem of the Strozzi Collection (in turn forged from an original in the Medici Collection), a second figure from the frieze of Nerva in the Forum Transitorium, and still another copied from a free-standing statue in the Vatican, the common denominator being only the "classicism" of all three. That one dates from the fourth century B.C., another from the second century A.D., and the third from the eighteenth century A.D. meant nothing. All were, or seemed, ancient and therefore excellent.

This sort of startling potpourri we see frequently in the designs of the Wedgwood factory. This was not the way of Josiah Wedgwood alone, however. He was but one of many. Classicism was in the air; it was *le dernier cri* and, most important, it sold. It would be a mistake to pretend that little money was made in the traffic of the remnants of "the glory that was Greece and the grandeur that was Rome." The Duke of Marlborough is said [3] to have paid Baron de Stosch £1000 for the cow of "Apollonides," a gem the authenticity of which has been questioned while its signature has been completely disproved. Michaelis states, [4] "No price was too high for the British purchasers; thirty-thousand scudi (about six-thousand guineas) were offered to Cardinal Furietti for the two black marble Centaurs which now stand in the Capitol; and Locke had already advanced a thousand zecchini (£600) for the Barberini candelabra but could not get permission to take them out of the country." Winckelmann wrote indignantly in a letter to a friend,[5] "Perhaps it will occur to some mad Englishman to have even Trajan's column transported to London."

Wedgwood was himself an astute and ambitious man. Before his entry into the field of competition in classical objects, he had improved his cream ware (later to be called Queen's Ware because of the patronage of Queen Charlotte) and had sold a set of it to the Empress Catherine of Russia. He began using classic designs in direct imitation of Greek vases, later he transposed the same motifs into black basalts and, finally, he developed a new medium in which to reproduce and modify the original subject matter, his justly famous and beautiful jasper ware.

Over the years he steadily enlarged his collection of subjects. If he juggled or, according to his lights, "improved," his classical originals, it was so that they would better suit the taste of the eighteenth-century market and thus sell better. For instance, if he clothed naked statues (he draped the herm of Priapus so that the god no longer lived up to his name), he did it to achieve salable goods that would not offend the morals of the English gentry. He wrote to his friend Flaxman (1790), ". . . The nude is so general in the works of the ancients, that it is very difficult to avoid the introduction of naked figures. On the other hand, it is absolutely necessary to do so [clothe the figures] or to keep the piece for our own use." He had no archaeological conscience to reproach him. Business was business, and besides Wedgwood was convinced that he was doing a fine job as he states in a letter to Erasmus Darwin, June 28, 1789, "I only pretend to have attempted to copy the antique forms, but not with absolute servility. I have attempted to preserve the style and spirit or if you please the elegant simplicity of antique forms, and so doing to introduce all the variety I was able, and this Sir William Hamilton assures me I may venture to do and that is the true way of copying the antique." However, in many cases, as will be seen later, "servile" imitation, or the exact use of a composition extracted from an ancient source, *can* be found among Wedgwood's designs.

The aims of this book are to determine the influences guiding the selection of Wedgwood's designs, to find the exact sources, as far as possible, of a cross section of the designs and to compare the originals and copies for differences. An attempt is made to discuss the influence of the milieu, of the buyers of his ware, and of Wedgwood's personal preferences on the selection of such designs. The sources are considered separately. These were usually casts, models, or books illustrating *objets d'art* of Greco-Roman attribution, although occasionally Wedgwood was able to avail himself of originals (such as gems) which were put at his disposal. The modification of the designs chosen is then discussed.

In order to elucidate the relative importance of the points mentioned above, it will be necessary to outline briefly the life of Josiah Wedgwood and the main characteristics of the Classic Revival. All controversial points in this regard, however, as well as the dating and authorship of the products of the Wedgwood factory, will be considered outside the limits of this book since they have been fully discussed elsewhere.

[1] Fiske Kimball, "Romantic Classicism in Architecture," *Gazette des Beaux-Arts,* Series VI, Vol. XXVI, 1944, p. 95.

[2] Laurentius Natter, *Treatise on the Ancient Method of Engraving on Precious Stone,* p. 5.

[3] Duffield Osborne, *Engraved Gems,* p. 181.

[4] Adolf Michaelis, *Ancient Marbles in Great Britain,* p. 87.

[5] Letter from Winckelmann to Muzel-Stosch, Feb. 26, 1768, quoted by Michaelis, *Marbles,* p. 87.

CLASSICAL WEDGWOOD DESIGNS

I

Josiah Wedgwood

JOSIAH WEDGWOOD, THE THIRTEENTH AND YOUNGEST CHILD of Thomas and Mary Springer Wedgwood, was baptized in the parish church of Burslem, Staffordshire, on July 12, 1730. The Wedgwoods were a prolific family, so that in spite of the possession of some property it was necessary for the cadet branches of the family to make a living by adopting the staple occupation of the district. Josiah Wedgwood's father as well as several of his uncles and cousins were potters.

When Josiah was nine, his father died and his school days were terminated. He at once began work at Burslem in the pottery of his brother Thomas and soon became an expert "thrower" on the wheel. At the age of eleven, an attack of smallpox greatly incapacitated him, affecting, in particular, his right knee. On November 11, 1744, when fifteen, he was apprenticed to his brother Thomas. The weakness of his knee soon compelled Josiah to abandon the thrower's bench and to occupy himself in other departments of the potter's art. He thus obtained a wider insight into the practical requirements of his craft.

Toward the end of his apprenticeship, he developed a love for experimentation which was not appreciated by his master and brother, who decided at the end of his term of indenture not to take him into partnership. At that point he joined, for a very short time, Thomas Alders and John Harrison in a small works at Cliff Bank near Stoke. He succeeded in improving the output of the small pottery, but his partners did not appreciate or recompense his efforts. He then entered partnership with Thomas Whieldon of Fenton and worked with him for about six years, until the close of 1758 when he decided to go into business for himself.

On December 30, 1758, he engaged his second cousin, Thomas Wedgwood of Worcester, a journeyman potter. It was probably during the first half of 1759 that Wedgwood became a master potter. His capital was small, and he took a small potwork in Burslem, part of the property of his cousins, called the Ivy House Works. Wedgwood introduced into his factory such modern industrial practices as the division of labor, and cleanliness and orderliness. He himself made most of the models and mixed the clays while also acting as clerk and warehouseman. In a short time his business became profitable, and in 1760 he was able to make a gift, double that of the other small potters, toward the establishment of a second free school. Very soon after this, Wedgwood paid much attention to the improvements of means of communication in the pottery district, giving evidence before a parliamentary committee in 1763, and subscribing £500 in 1765 toward the making of new roads. Later he took an important part in the development of the local canal system. In 1763 he found it necessary to find additional accommodations and rented the Brick House and Works in Burslem, where he remained until his final removal to Etruria in 1773.

Some time between 1762 and 1765 he was appointed "Potter to Her Majesty" for his cream ware service. On January 25, 1764, at Astbury in Cheshire, Wedgwood married a distant cousin, Sarah, the daughter of Richard Wedgwood of Spen Green. Seven children were the result of this union, three sons and four daughters. In 1776, Thomas Wedgwood, who had been employed since 1759, was taken into partnership. In the same year Wedgwood pur-

chased for £3000 a site called Ridge House Estate, between Burslem and Stoke-on-Trent for a new factory and residence. Later on
he added to this and built a village for his workmen which he
called Etruria, a mansion called Etruria Hall, and an extensive
and well-equipped potwork. The new Etruria factory was opened
formally on June 13, 1769, just ten years after Josiah had started
on his own.

During this period, he was active in public affairs, helping to
settle the question of the Trent and Mersey Canal and in 1777
acting as its first treasurer. In October, 1766, he closed his London
showroom in Charles Street and in 1768 opened a larger place in
Newport Street, St. Martin's Lane. In 1774 the establishment
moved to Greek Street, Soho. In 1768 his weak right leg was
amputated, and in November of the same year terms of partnership with Thomas Bentley of Liverpool were settled. Their association was only in the production of ornamental ware, as his
partnership with his cousin Thomas was in useful wares. The
friendship and partnership with Bentley continued until Bentley's
death in 1780. In 1773, Wedgwood started experimenting with the
ware known later as "jasper" but produced no vases in this material until after the death of Bentley. In 1774, on the order of
Catherine II of Russia, he finished the famous Russian cream ware
dinner service. In 1783, he was elected a Fellow of the Royal
Society and contributed two papers on chemical subjects and three
on the construction and use of the pyrometer, an invention for
determining and registering high temperatures by the measure-
ment of the shrinkage suffered by cylinders of prepared clay in
the furnace. On May 4, 1786, Wedgwood was elected a Fellow of
the Society of Antiquaries. The year 1790 saw the original issue of
Wedgwood's copy of the Barberini or Portland vase. In the same
year he retired to Etruria Hall and diverted himself by collecting
books, engravings, and objects of natural history. After a brief
illness, Josiah Wedgwood died at Etruria Hall on January 3, 1795,
at the age of sixty-four and was buried in the Stoke-on-Trent
churchyard. He left a fortune of £500,000 and a flourishing business.

II

Wedgwood Wares

———

THE WARES MADE AT CLIFF BANK POTTERY WERE MOTTLED, cloudy, and tortoise shell, glazed with lead or salt and shining black of very good quality. Also, tea services, jugs and other articles were made in what was then styled "blue-scratched" ware. This was a white body on which were scratched by a sharp nail, flowers, Chinese-like pagodas and mandarins which were then dusted with ground zaffre, an impure oxide of cobalt. With Whieldon it is supposed that he improved the green ware, but Barnard thinks that the prized "cauliflowers" and "pineapple" ware always attached with Whieldon's name were not produced until Wedgwood went into business himself. In support of this hypothesis, moulds, blocks, and trials were discovered at Etruria in 1925, among which were the salt-glazed pattern block moulds of the "cauliflower" and "pineapple" pieces. Especially choice Whieldon pieces were small oval snuffboxes of dead white glaze decorated on the lid and sides with little flowers enamelled in blue, red, and yellow.

First wares at the Ivy House Works were green glazed wares, snuffboxes, perforated and streaked dessert plates, knife-hafts, tortoise shell and melon plates. On white stone ware tiles for fireplaces and on teapots occur Wedgwood's first experimental relief work. He then turned his efforts toward the improvement of cream-colored ware, and by the close of 1761 he had brought his cream ware to a certain degree of perfection. The body had a lightness, the glaze a brilliancy hitherto unknown, and further-more the forms in which it appeared were new. The forms of the chief pieces such as tureens, sauceboats, and saltcellars, were modelled from natural objects, that is, shells, leaves, and the husks and seed valves of plants. Enamelling was in soft and subdued colors. Later, Sadler and Green of Liverpool decorated the cream ware with prints.

The success of the cream-colored ware was immediate and wide-spread in spite of the fact that the area in which the potteries were situated was somewhat off the map and communications extraordinarily difficult. In 1765, for instance, we hear of a friend who reported that at a dinner with Lord Gower, Wedgwood's "potworks were the subject of conversation for some time, the Cream Color table services in particular. . . . His Lordship said that nothing of the sort could exceed them for fine glaze."

Josiah Wedgwood had achieved such acclaim that in the same year he received his first order from Royalty, a caudle service for Queen Charlotte, wife of George III. Josiah jokingly said that he obtained this commission "because nobody else would undertake it," but in fact it was probably due far more to his pre-eminence in the production of cream-colored tableware. As a result of the commission, he was allowed to style himself potter to the Queen and to christen this product Queen's Ware.

Between 1766 and 1768 the perfection of the fine black ware called basalt, was accomplished. It was this black ware that was used as a foundation for a style of encaustic painting in colors, mainly in red and black, in the style which was termed "Etruscan," i.e., inspired by the paintings on the vases found in Italy and brought back by Sir William Hamilton. The six famous vases thrown at the opening of the Etruria Works on June 18, 1769, were basalt and decorated with encaustic painting. Bentley is supposed to have been the moving spirit in the making of the vases and Wedgwood's ruling passion for a time was the perfection of these vases and the encaustic painting of them. Almost all the shapes and designs found in jasper have their replicas in basalt though many of the large vases in basalt were never attempted in jasper.

The first mention of the "white body" later to be called "jasper" is in July, 1774, but the year 1775 is usually considered the year in which small articles were first made. The biggest technical problem to overcome was the tendency of the colored background to "bleed" through. As it is ruefully stated by Wedgwood to Bentley July 9, 1776, "In some things the blue shade which our ground is so apt to cast through the thin parts of the white, may be of advantage to the subject, as in the Armour by the side of the conquer'd Province . . . But when the naked part of the Figure is penetrated with the color of the ground, it is generally injurious— see the poor Queen's nose and many other Cameo's."

Though usually left with its natural matt, it was capable of taking a high polish. This can be seen on the grounds and bevelled edges of the smaller cameos and intaglios in more direct imitation of natural stratified stones. Jasper was made in several tones of blue, yellow, lilac, green, and black, each color having several modifications. It was made in two ways, one known as "solid jasper," the other as "jasper dip." In the first case the entire substance of the white body was colored by the metallic oxide used, and in the second only the surface was stained. Jasper dip was invented in 1785 in order to obtain a higher quality in color rather than to economize. In 1781, Wedgwood produced ornamental jasper vases, and the first ones were shown to the public in 1782 at the Greek Street establishment in Soho. Cameos, medallions, plaques, and tablets as well as *dejeuner* pieces were made in this material. Many of the smaller cameos were and are set in jewelry, furniture, etc.

Other of his products were variegated wares of two kinds, a solid agate colored throughout its entire substance by means of the association in bands, twists, stripes, and waves of clays in different hues and a type colored only on the surface, the body being of cream ware. Handles and plinths usually were left in their natural state. Under the names rosso antico, cane-colored and bamboo ware, Wedgwood included a number of bodies of the terra-cotta type. They had a dead dry surface and were distinctly porous. These bodies were sometimes used in conjunction with basalts, two of them often being associated in the same vase, sometimes decorated with reliefs in white paste. Red and chocolate color, red relief on black basalt, white on chocolate, purplish-black on white, and dull sage green on cane color, all afforded satisfactory contrasts.

The first catalogue of ornamental ware was published in 1773, and the listing is as follows: [1]

Catalogue of cameos, intaglios, medals, bas-reliefs, busts, small statues, vases, etc. *London, 1773.* Sold by Cadel, in the Strand; Robson, New Bond Street; and Parker, printseller, Cornhill. 12°, pp. 60.

This was the first edition of the catalogue, for which Bentley is said to have written the introduction.

The subsequent editions were issued, at intervals, with but slight alterations in the title:

1774. 2nd ed.—A French translation, 8°, pp. 82, was issued in London, same year.
1775. 3rd ed.—A reissue of the 2nd ed.; with 6 pp. added and a woodcut of the inkstand.
1777. 4th ed.—In English.
1778. A Dutch translation, published in Amsterdam.
1779. 5th ed.—In English—A French edition, *London;* and a German translation, with a view of the showroom in Soho, engraved in colour, *Leipzig,* were published same year.
1787. 6th ed., under the following title:
Catalogue of cameos, intaglios, medals, bas-reliefs, busts, and small statues; with a general account of tablets, vases, escritoires, and other ornamental and useful articles. The whole formed in different kinds of porcelain and terra-cotta, chiefly after the antique and the finest models of modern artists. By Josiah Wedgwood, F.R.S., potter to Her Majesty, and to His Royal Highness the Duke of York and Albany. Sold at his rooms in Greek Street, Soho, London,

and at his manufactory in Staffordshire. The sixth edition
with additions. *Etruria,* 1787. 8°, pp. 78; with two plates
engraved in blue steaple.
1788. A last French edition. 8°, pp. 89; with 2 pls.

In 1817 there appeared under the title *Museum Etruriae; or a
catalogue of cameos, etc. By the late Josiah Wedgwood,* a reprint
of the 1787 edition of the *Catalogue* printed for James Boardman,
to which a brief history of the art of pottery in England, and a
description of the Barberini, or Portland, vase were added. It contained 149 pages with engravings of the Portland vase.

Any of these *Catalogues* are now difficult to find. Even rarer,
however, are the *Queen's Ware Catalogues* the first of which was
published in 1774. These have been reprinted in *Old Wedgwood,*
1942 (pp. 109 ff.), with plates and in Barnard, *Chats on Wedgwood Ware* (pp. 94 ff.), with plates. Barnard, however, dates his
Catalogue ca. 1770–1780 and states that it is in French.

1 Louis M. E. Solon, *Ceramic Literature; An Analytical Index,* pp. 444 ff.

III

Books and Patrons

———

THE FRIENDS AND PATRONS OF WEDGWOOD MUST HERE BE
mentioned since many of his designs were obtained from private
collections and libraries. The names of Lord Cathcart (ambas-
sador to Russia), Sir William Hamilton, Sir Watkin Williams
Wynne, and James Stuart recur often in his letters, not only as
customers but as being interested in the enlargement of his
classical art vocabulary. The list of cameos and intaglios in the
first edition of the Catalogue proves how diligently Wedgwood
and his partner had applied themselves to the study of antique
gems. They purchased impressions of these from Tassie, the well-
known modeller of gems, in sulphur wax and a white paste or
plaster composition; or more generally, as at a later date, modelled
from the gems themselves, such as those in the possession of the
Duke of Marlborough, Lord Bessborough, Lord Clanbrassil, Sir
William Hamilton, Sir Watkin Williams Wynne, Sir Roger Newdigate, Mr. Anson, Mr. Folley, Stuart and others.

Sir Watkin Williams Wynne was one of Wedgwood's earliest
and most munificent patrons. He contributed 172 intaglios and
173 gems or cameos to Wedgwood's first lists.

Wedgwood and Bentley presented Hamilton with a bas-relief

11

of the *Crowning of a Citharist,* then known as the *Apotheosis of Homer,* as a token of gratitude for his help, and he replied with more suggestions for designs to be taken from the publication of his antiquities, a copy of which he had presented them. He had also sent them casts of antique subjects besides lending them cameos and gems and being instrumental in opening many collections to their use.

These are but a few examples of the manner in which the nobility aided one of their favorite craftsmen. For it was only the nobility who possessed the monetary means to collect antiquities or even to buy the products of the Wedgwood factory.

Another and still more important element in the quest for classical subject matter and materials was the use of books and prints. Wedgwood and Bentley steeped themselves in classical lore and mythology and were undoubtedly familiar with every important work on antiquities published up to that time. Though the books to which one is usually referred as the sources for designs are those of the Comte de Caylus, Sir William Hamilton and d'Hancarville, and Montfaucon, in order to understand fully the origins of the Wedgwood designs one must realize that the potter was familiar with many and varied publications. That the partners used the collection at the British Museum is attested by a letter from Wedgwood to Bentley, November 3, 1768, "I shall expect *written instruction* what books I am to buy and what books I am to see at the Museum . . ."

Meteyard comments, "There is every reason to infer that both Bentley and his friend were well acquainted with the works of LaChausse, Laurent, Beger, Montfaucon, Dempster, Gori, Winckelmann as well as those of the Count de Caylus."

Michelange LaChausse [1] (who often went under the Latinized version of his name, Causeus) was a Frenchman who was born in Paris toward the end of the seventeenth century but lived in Rome. He published many works of first rank on the antiquities of Rome. The ones which Wedgwood probably knew were *Le Gemme Antiche Figurate,* Rome and Paris, 1720, and the enlargement and revision of **Picture antiche delle grotte di Roma e del**

Sepolcro de Nasoni, Rome, 1706, by Pietro Sante Bartoli, engraver, and Pietro Bellori, which appeared with a Latin text and further engravings by Francesco Bartoli, son of Pietro, in 1738 and 1750.

If Meteyard refers to Henri Laurent, author of *Le Musée Francais* and later *Le Musée Royal,* in her list of works Wedgwood may have known, it is evident that she did not realize that these works did not appear until 1803–1809 and 1816–1818 respectively.

Laurentius Beger (1653–1705)[2] was a scholar in the field of antique coins and gems. He was custodian of the Cabinet of Antiques at Heidelberg and of the collection of ancient art at Berlin. His *Thesaurus Brandenburgicus* (1696) contained a large selection of ancient coins and gems with commentary.

The manuscript work of Thomas Dempster,[3] a Scotsman who had lived in Bologna and died in 1625, was published by Thomas Coke, later Lord Leicester, in Florence, 1723–1724. This work was a compilation of information about Etruria and the Etruscans with an appendix by Filippo Buonarroti. Michaelis says of it,[4] "The book thus produced . . . has acquired a heightened interest inasmuch as it has been the innocent cause of that foolish Etruscomania which prevailed for many years in Italy—a startling example of the length to which that people can be led by misdirected local patriotism in conjunction with confused, uncritical learning." This and the works of Caylus were definitely responsible for the "Etruscan" vases of Wedgwood.

Antonio Francesco Gori (1691–1757),[5] was a priest and professor in Florence. He published not only Greek and Roman inscriptions but also six volumes on coins and gems in his *Museum Florentinum* containing the works of art in the private collections in Florence.

Johann Joachim Winckelmann (1717–1768),[6] was the son of a cobbler who studied the classics under the foremost teachers of the times and whose main aim in life was the study of art, in particular, Classical Art. He joined the Church of Rome in order to do so more freely. In Rome he studied gems, the excavations of Herculaneum and Pompeii, the temples of Paestum and Girgenti, and the works in the Vatican Museum. His written works are: *Thoughts on the Imitation of Greek Works in Painting and Sculpture* (1755), *History of Ancient Art* (1764), a descriptive *Catalogue of the de Stosch Collection of Gems* (1760), and two volumes of *Monumenti Antichi Inediti* (1776). His history of art is the earliest book in which the development of the art of Egypt, Phoenicia, Persia, Greece, and Rome is set forth in connection with the development of political life and civilization. His book of monuments described more than two hundred works of ancient art, mainly reliefs on sarcophagi, in explanation that the scenes were derived from mythology and not from the everyday life of the times.

Bernard de Montfaucon (1655–1741)[7] was a French Benedictine monk whose most famous work, *Antiquité Expliquée,* was a vast treasury of classical antiquities first published in five volumes, then in ten parts in 1719, and later with a five-volume supplement. It was translated into English, and it is possible that Wedgwood knew that edition. It supplied a comprehensive summary of all antiquarian learning of the age. Its plates were often taken from other publications.

The Comte de Caylus,[8] after a military career, studied the monuments of Asia Minor, Constantinople, and Rome. He spent four-fifths of his large income on the patronage of archaeology, filling his house with ancient works of art three times and on each occasion presenting them to royal collections. He published a large number of monuments in the seven-volume work *Recueil d'Antiquités* (1752–1767). Included were only those works that he himself had, and in this way he was more discriminating in his judgments than Montfaucon. His numerous memoirs, which he presented to the Academy in and after 1744, deal in a scientific spirit with the works of ancient art. He transformed his home into a laboratory[9] to study ancient painting and to recreate antique works, especially the glazes and painting on vases.

The names of Sir William Hamilton, British minister to Naples, and the French adventurer d'Hancarville[10] are joined in the publication of the *Antiquités Grecques, Etrusques et Romaines*

. . . *du Cabinet de M. Hamilton,* Naples, 1766–1767. There is a
second edition of 1801–1803. This collection consisted mostly of
later specimens of vases which were greatly overvalued.[11]

In August, 1770, the books belonging to the firm [12] were set
down by Wedgwood as follows:

Hamilton's Etruscan Antiquities
Gemms Delin, by Elizabeth Cherron, small Fol[a].
Stuart's Athens
Count Caylus's Antiq[s]. 3 vols.
Temple of the Muses, Fol[a].
Rossi's Statues, Fol[a].
Iconologie Historique, De la Fosse, Fol[a].

and to these were soon added

Spence's Polymeitis
Museum Odescaleum, sive Thesaurus Antiq. Gemmarum a
   Bartolo, Rome, 1750
Maffie [sic] and Agostini's Gemms, Fol[a].
Gravelot's Antiquities
De Wilde gemme Antique, 1703
Agostini, by Gronovius
Perrico's Statues
Ficoroni's Gemms
Middleton's Antiquities

All of these books deal with antique *objets d'art* and are profusely
illustrated. They will be discussed briefly in the following para-
graphs.

"Gemms Delin by Elizabeth Cherron" no doubt refers to
Pierres Gravées Tirées des Principaux Cabinets de France (no
date or place of publication) by Elisabeth Sophie Chéron (1648–
1711),[13] which had forty-one plates engraved by her and is considered the principal work of this talented Frenchwoman.

"Stuart's Athens" refers to the work of James "Athenian" Stuart
(1713–1788),[14] a painter and architect who, in the company of
Nicholas Revett, an architect and draftsman, went to Greece.
Their visit there resulted in a great work of permanent value, the
Antiquities of Athens Measured and Delineated (1762–1830).
That he was a good friend of Wedgwood is attested by Meteyard.

The "Temple of the Muses" is another eighteenth-century publication. The title in Dutch, the language in which it was printed
at Amsterdam in 1733, is *De Tempel der Zang-Godinnen* (with
titles in French and English). The plates are by a famous engraver,
Bernard Picart,[15] called "le Romain." It contains sixty plates illustrating various myths and legends of classical times. There is an
English edition of 1733, in the Chatsworth library.

The abbreviated title "Rossi's Statues" refers to the *Raccolta di
Statue Antiche e Moderne*, Rome, 1704, by Domenico de Rossi.
"Iconologie Historique, De la Fosse" is the short title given to the
work of Jean Charles De la Fosse, *Nouvelle Iconologie Historique*,
Paris, 1768, which contains plates of emblems, trophies, medal-
lions, and various other decorative works.

"Spence's Polymeitis" refers to the work of Joseph Spence
(1699–1768)[16] which is a treatise on classical art and mythology.
Spence was so highly thought of that he was one of the few com-
moners admitted to the Society of the Dilettanti when it was first
formed.[17]

The next book on the list, "Museum Odescaleum . . ." with
engravings by Bartoli, was the publication of the gems belonging
to the family Odescalchi, published by Monaldini, Rome, 1751
(not 1750, as has been claimed).

"Maffie and Agostini's Gemms" and "Agostini, by Gronovius"
refer to different editions of Lionardo Agostini's *Gemme Antiche*,
the first part of which was published in 1636–1657, and the second
part in 1670. Agostini[18] was a celebrated seventeenth-century
antiquary, a native of Siena, employed by Cardinal Barberini.
Maffei and Rossi published an enlarged edition in 1707, and Jacob
Gronovius, a Latin translation in 1685 in Amsterdam.

"Gravelot's Antiquities" is a collection of engravings and a text
dealing with iconology or symbolical representations, by Hubert
François Gravelot (1699–1773),[19] an engraver. This work has appeared in various editions since 1765, and as Gravelot died before
it was finished, Cochin carried it on. It was published by Lattré
under the title *Almanach Iconologique*.

Jacob de Wilde[20] was a Dutchman who lived in Amsterdam

and was extremely interested in numismatics. He gathered together a library and cabinet of antiquities and medals. The
work owned by Wedgwood was probably his *Gemmae Selectae
Antiquae,* Amsterdam, 1703.

"Ficoroni's Gemms" is the *Gemmae Antiquae Litteratae,* Rome,
Monaldini, 1757, by Francisco Ficoroni,[21] an antiquary living in
Rome, who supplied drawings from antique gems for a few
crowns. "Middleton's Antiquities" is probably the *Germana
Quaedam Antiquitatis Eruditae Monumenta,* 1745, an account of
the antiquities bought in Rome by Conyers Middleton,[22] a famous
English divine.

The only publication on the inventory which cannot be definitely identified is "Perrico's Statues." It is the opinion of the
author that, in view of the misspelling of other names and titles
on the list, this is a mistake. There is a François or Francisco
Perrier (1590–1650)[23] who published a collection of engravings
of statues in Rome, *Statuae Antiquae Centum, . . .* Francisco
Perrier, Rome, 1638. This might possibly be the book as it contains plates of such famous statues as the Farnese Flora and Farnese Heracles which Wedgwood knew.

It seems that two publications with which Wedgwood seemed
to be acquainted are missing from the list. He may have seen them
at the British Museum or borrowed them from patrons and
friends. But no list of books known to Wedgwood would be complete without the *Admiranda Romanarum Antiquitatum ac
Veteris Sculpturae Vestigia,* Rome, 1693, and the *Veterum
Sepulcra,* 1728, both authored by Pietro Sante Bartoli and Bellori.
A third publication is the La Chausse and Francisco Bartoli edition of Bellori and Pietro Bartoli's work on ancient paintings
called in the 1738 and 1750 editions, *Picturae Antiquae Crypto-
rum Romanorum et Sepulcri Nasonum.*

[1] *Biographie Universelle* (Michaud), VIII, pp. 48 ff.
[2] Sir John E. Sandys, *A History of Classical Scholarship,* II, p. 368.
[3] *Ibid.,* II, p. 340.
[4] Michaelis, *Marbles,* pp. 60 ff.

[5] Sandys, *op. cit.,* II, p. 380.

[6] *Ibid.,* III, pp. 21 ff.

[7] *Ibid.,* II, pp. 385 ff.

[8] *Ibid.,* II, pp. 390 ff.

[9] Louis Hautecoeur, *Rome et la Renaissance de l'Antiquité à la Fin du XVIIIe Siècle,* Fascicule 105, p. 25.

[10] *Biographie Universelle* (Michaud), XVIII, pp. 415 ff.

[11] Henry B. Walters, "Vases of the Latest Period," *Catalogue of the Greek and Etruscan Vases in the British Museum,* IV, p. 3.

[12] Meteyard, *Life,* II, p. 231, n. 2; *Wedgwood and His Works,* p. 39, n. 2.

[13] *Biographie Universelle* (Michaud), VIII, p. 92.

[14] Sandys, *op. cit.,* II, p. 432.

[15] *Biographie Universelle* (Michaud), XXXIII, pp. 180 ff.

[16] Sandys, *op. cit.,* II, p. 411.

[17] *Ibid.,* II, p. 431.

[18] *Biographie Universelle* (Michaud), I, pp. 235 ff.

[19] *Ibid.,* XVII, pp. 391 ff.

[20] *Ibid.,* XLIV, p. 607.

[21] Michaelis, *Ancient Marbles,* p. 58.

[22] *Dictionary of National Biography,* XXXVII, p. 348.

[23] *Biographie Universelle* (Michaud), XXXII, pp. 535 ff.

IV

Specific Sources of Designs

ACHILLES

MANY SCENES FROM THE LIFE OF ACHILLES WERE USED BY Wedgwood. One of the sources for these is the Luna marble disc [1] surrounded by mosaic in the Capitoline Museum. Now in the *Stanze Terrene a Sinistra,* it was given to the museum by Pope Benedict XIV.[2] The ambo of St. Maria Aracoeli of which this was originally a part was made by the brothers Cosmati in the thirteenth century and at that time the relief band must have been set with mosaic. The band is of peculiar form and has been regarded as a wellhead, or puteal. It is dated as early medieval or between the fourth and eighth centuries A.D.

The individual designs on the disc are good and the actions clearly delineated, but the workmanship is rough [3] and at times the treatment is schematic. Notable is the use of trees and columns as marks of division between the scenes.

The band carries the following scenes: [4]

1. The childbed of Thetis.
2. Thetis dipping Achilles into the river Styx.
3. Thetis delivering the infant to the mother or sister of Cheiron.

4. The female centaur carrying Achilles on her back in pursuit of a lion.
5. Achilles at Scyros.
6. Individual combat before the walls of Troy.
7. Achilles dragging the body of Hector around the walls of Troy.

In the adaptation of this series, Wedgwood does not use all the scenes in the same plaque or on the same vase. He uses, rather, individual motifs or pairs of them.

Plate 1. Birth and dipping of Achilles. *Wedgwood.*

1. *The Birth and dipping of Achilles.* Plate 1. Illustrated in Meteyard, *Life of Josiah Wedgwood,* II, p. 592.[5] The design is attributed to Pacetti,[6] although it was once assigned to Flaxman. Meteyard says,[7] "In simplicity and truth of conception and in the grace of the female and infantile figures, it is worthy of the great master [Wedgwood]. It is also true to that canon of his art—and of the best age of Greek art too—that one idea should govern the whole and that the field of representation be not overcrowded." In the face of the attribution of the original disc to the fourth to eighth centuries A.D., certainly not the best period of Greek art, the statement above, after comparison of pottery version and original, is not actually so much a tribute to the taste of Wedgwood as to the skill and craftsmanship of Pacetti, who in his adaptation was capable of giving a "Golden Age" air to a lively medieval work.

2. *Thetis delivering infant to Centaur, and Centaur, Achilles on back, hunting the lion.* Plates 2 and 3. Illustrated and discussed

in Meteyard, *Wedgwood and His Works,* Pl. VI and Plate XXVI.
The plaque is blue jasper; white relief; measures 18½ inches by
6½ inches; date 1790–1795; artist, Pacetti. Here, however, the

Plate 2. Thetis delivering Achilles to Centaur and Achilles on back
of Centaur hunting the lion. *Wedgwood.*

Plate 3. Thetis delivering Achilles to Centaur and Achilles on back
of Centaur hunting the lion. *Source.*

evaluation has changed. Meteyard now says, "The field of the
design is rather bare; but portions are nicely undercut, and great
expression is conveyed in the face of the Centaur. An interesting
plaque, but not of the highest quality in either colour or subject."

It is true that the spaces between the figures are wider than in
the marble puteal, but they are no wider than those in the Wedgwood version of *The Birth and Dipping of Achilles.* The subject
matter is certainly classical, and it has been executed for Wedg-

wood by the same man, Pacetti. Why, then, this criticism? It must
go unexplained. It is interesting to note that in this tablet the sex
of the Centaur has suffered a change. It certainly is not female,
yet it lacks the identifying attributes of the male sex. One is, however, led to believe that it is male because of muscular development of arms and shoulders. In its present neutral state it would
certainly offend no one.

Plate 4. Achilles in Scyros among the daughters of Lycomedes. *Source.*

3. *Achilles in Scyros among the daughters of Lycomedes.* Plate
4. Illustrated and discussed in Meteyard, *Memorials of Wedgwood,* Pl. XIV. There is a replica, perhaps the same vase, in the
Boston Museum of Fine Arts, No. L. Pink jasper vase; white relief;
border beneath frieze, of checker pattern; height 13 inches; date
1788–1798. It is stated that the "Subject . . . 'Achilles and the
Daughters of Lycomedes' [was] taken from a tablet in Rome by
Angelo Dalmazzoni, one of the best Italian artists of the time."
Meteyard, *Life,* II, p. 590, is evidently not aware of the fact that
this particular version is part of the "whole life of Achilles from

his mother Thetis in childbed to his triumph over Hector" assigned to Pacetti.

4. *Achilles dragging Hector around the walls of Troy,* Plate 5. Illustrated in Meteyard, *Wedgwood and His Works,* Pl. XV. Dark green jasper; white relief; 4¾ inches by 3 inches; egg and tongue border. Meteyard lists this subject under *Cameos* and goes on to say, "Most of the cameos are derived from pastes by Tassie of antique gemms. . . . The subject, derived from Homer's *Iliad,* Book XXIV, is 'The body of Hector dragged at the car of Achilles.'

Plate 5. Achilles dragging Hector around the walls of Troy. *Source.*

The original is in carnelian . . ." There are two carnelian gems of this subject mentioned in the catalogue of Tassie impressions; [8] however, the details of this pottery cameo match so closely the final episode in this series, that it is thought to have been inspired by the Luna marble disc in the Capitoline Museum. The number of horses, the position of the horses, the brandishing of the sword by Achilles, the attitude of the body of the dead Hector, and last of all the carry-over of three piers from the wall of Troy point to the stone version. An alternative explanation which can be offered is that the disc inspired a gem engraver to copy this episode, that Tassie took a cast of it and then sold it to Wedgwood. Pichler, an eighteenth-century gem engraver, is known to have executed more than twelve times [9] the subject of Achilles dragging the body of Hector about the walls of Troy.

In comparing the puteal and the pottery versions, the differences most apparent in the Wedgwood treatment are that the
figures are more graceful and the drapery has been better delineated. The original artist was satisfied with a few incised lines, as
in the drapery of Thetis and the ribs of the lion. Pacetti has tran-
scribed this artistic shorthand into round folds and rippling
muscles. The figures in the older relief are not well-proportioned,

Plate 6. Achilles in Scyros among the daughters of Lycomedes.
Wedgwood plaque.

having that peculiar dumpy look of late Roman art. There is in
the over-all effect less of of the lively expression found in the
medieval tablet because of the tendency to prettify and classicize.
There are such minor changes as replacement by a staff of a tree
in the hand of the reclining figure representing the river Styx and
the spaces between figures and scenes are greater in the jasper.
These are, however, only minor changes. To sum up, the difference between original and copy is more in concept than in detail.

There are two other versions of *Achilles in Scyros,* Plate 6. The
first of these to be discussed is illustrated in Meteyard, *Wedgwood
and His Works,* Pl. III and XII. Black jasper; white relief; 19
inches by 7 inches; 1790. She says of it, "This bas-relief was
modelled in Flaxman's atelier in Rome by Devaere for Wedgwood. The latter, guided by prints, chose this and other subjects
for modelling." The source for this design is a sarcophagus illustrated in Robert, *Die Antiken Sarkophag-Reliefs,* II, Pl. XVIII,

nos. 29 and 29₁. No. 29 is a cut taken from Winckelmann, *Monumenti Antichi Inediti*, 1767, I, Fig. 87; he identifies the subject matter as part of the Meleager cycle. No. 29₁ is taken from Raoul-Rochette, *Monumens Inédits, Grecs, Etrusque et Romains*, 1826–1833, Pl. X B 2. Winckelmann saw it in the Villa Albani; it was then reported to be in the Palazzo Nari and finally more accurately drawn by Raoul-Rochette while in the possession of an

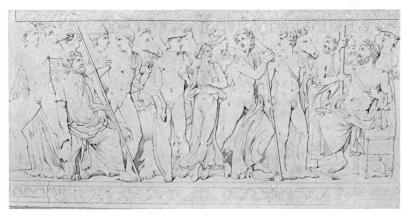

Plate 7. The Sacrifice of Iphigenia. *Source.*

art dealer, Vescovali.[10] The composition of the Devaere design tallies with the Winckelmann version; hence it can be assumed that it was from this print that the artist worked. The figure of Achilles is central; he brandishes a sword in his right hand and a shield in his left. A group of three men are at his left. Two of these are about to draw their swords. Deidameia is on her knees and clutches the right knee of Achilles; her drapery billows behind her. Just to the left and in back, a sister is waving more drapery. This pose is exaggerated in the pottery version wherein she seems to be engaged in a scarf dance as she pulls the cloth over her head. She is not whipping the chiton of Achilles off him, for his is slipping down his right leg. At the extreme left is a group of three sisters in agitated positions. Both Raoul-Rochette and Winckelmann have two more female figures at the left; these have been omitted in some pottery copies presumably for the sake

of greater symmetry. Other slight differences exist. The slipping
chiton of Achilles in the Wedgwood has not slipped so far that
decency is offended. What was a couch in the original is a table
heaped with a helmet, vase, beads, and cloth in the jasper. In this
case, it seems that the eighteenth-century workmanship is of a
higher caliber, as the sarcophagus was described as being of "lavoro
mediocre." [11]

The third use of the *Achilles in Scyros* theme, **Plate 7**, is illustrated in Meteyard, *Life of Josiah Wedgwood*, II, p. 591, although
there it is called the *Sacrifice of Iphigenia*. Pacetti is credited with
the working of this plaque, the source of which has been recog-
nized [12] as the erroneously [13] named sarcophagus of Alexander
Severus and Julia Mammaea [14] in the Capitoline Museum. It is a
sarcophagus with reliefs on all sides, and Wedgwood utilized those
on three of them. This sepulchral monument was found in the
year 1582 or shortly before then by Fabrizio Lazaro in the "Monte
del Grano" three miles from Porta S. Giovanni between the Via
Latina and the Via Labicana.[15] It was moved to its present position in the Stanza Terrena a Dritta in 1817.[16] *Achilles in Scyros* is
on the front.[17] Just to the right of center, Achilles is brandishing
a sword, his woman's chiton slipping. Deidameia, as though to
restrain him lays both her hands on his shoulders from behind.
One of her sisters in a long girt chiton springs away to the left
with a gesture of alarm. The misnomer of the *Sacrifice of Iphigenia*
is probably due to this figure arrangement in which the sword is
thought to be directed at the sister. On each side is a king with an
attendant group. Jones states,[18] "The figures, slender and well
modelled, especially in contrast to the figures on the lid, are ultimately derived from later Attic standards. For the period (third
century A.D.) . . . the work is exceptionally good. . . . Additional charm is given by the excellent preservation of the monument." The pottery version is in lower relief than the original,
and there is therefore much less play of light and dark. The figures
in the original seem livelier and less fixed in space because of the
deeper relief. The translation into pottery is quite exact considering the differences in material.

The design taken from the back is *Priam begging for the body of Hector from Achilles,* Plate 8. It is illustrated in Meteyard, *Wedgwood and His Works,* p. 1, and Meteyard, *Choice Examples of Wedgwood Art,* Pl. VIII, and two excellent copies are in the Walters Art Gallery in Baltimore. One is in black jasper, white relief; originally in the Horace Townsend collection, 1914. The other is green jasper, white relief; originally in the Sibson collec-

Plate 8. Priam begging for the body of Hector from Achilles. *Wedgwood plaque.*

tion, 1877; W. D. Holt, 1892; L. Huth, 1905; Harding, 1911. This also was modelled for Wedgwood by Pacetti in Rome. This side of the sarcophagus differs from the front in having no central group but rather a movement all in one direction and in being much rougher in execution.[19] On the extreme right is seated Achilles in an attitude of grief. Before him kneels the aged Priam who is kissing the right hand of Achilles. Behind Priam stands a two-horse chariot. On the left, the scene is completed by Priam's wagon with his gifts. There are various figures of Greeks and two Trojans, distinguished by their long-sleeved tunics, trousers, and Phrygian caps. It is interesting to note here that an eighteenth-century gem,[20] a sardonyx belonging to a Mr. F. Egerton, signed by Marchant and representing the group of Priam and Achilles, has also been used for small cameos by Wedgwood but has been adapted from a similar sarcophagus in the Louvre.[21] In the library at Mellerstain, Berwickshire (1770–1778), the brothers Adam use this composition, but in reverse, as part of the wall decoration.[22]

The Wedgwood medallion of *Two Warriors and a Horse,* Plates 9a and 10, seems to have been adapted from the group at the left angle of the left short side of the sarcophagus, representing *Achilles taking leave of Lycomedes.* Illustrated in Meteyard, *Wedgwood and His Works,* Pl. VIII, no. 1. Pale blue jasper; white reliefs; 6⅝ inches in diameter. A young warrior with a

Plate 9a, 9b. Warriors and Horses. *Source.*

helmet, cuirass, shield, and spear stands with Achilles, who has his right hand on his horse's head, his left grasping his chlamys which falls from the left shoulder across the back and around the right thigh. His sword is seen on the right, underneath the horse and between the two men who both wear high boots. Miss Meteyard says of it, "This bas-relief does not appear in catalogues; but there can be little doubt that it is a copy from the cast of a fragment by Phidias modelled by Flaxman for Wedgwood Sept. 6, 1782 and charged 10s. 6d. in a bill of that period, now in the Wedgwood Museum. It has all the simplicity of treatment, truth, and accuracy of Greek sculpture at its meridian. The cast may be from some fragments of antique sculpture sent to this country by Sir Wm. Hamilton." The detailed similarities of this jasper ware and the sarcophagus mentioned above, however, are inescapable: the drape

Plate 10. Two Warriors and a Horse. *Wedgwood plaque.*

of the chlamys of Achilles, the postures of both youths, the pointed edges of their boots, the peculiar cutting off of the horse, and the position of the hand of Achilles on the head of the horse leave

Plate 11. Three Warriors and a Horse. *Wedgwood plaque.*

little doubt regarding the source. This is a good example of the lifting and use of part of a design without regard to its meaning in the general context of the original monument.

Three Warriors and a Horse, Plates 9b and 11, illustrated in Meteyard, *Choice Examples of Wedgwood Art,* Pl. IX, is taken from the other small side of the sarcophagus. Use of the entire compositions of both small sides of this sarcophagus by Wedgwood can be seen in Hannover.[23] It might be further conjectured that since Pacetti worked the other two sides, these are also a product of the atelier at Rome and by him. The placing of the figures on the medallion in the "meridian" of Greek sculpture can be set aside in view of the dating of the monument in the third century A.D.,[24] yet the confusion is understandable when it is recalled that they were modelled from Attic standards.

Plate 12. Aesculapius and Hygeia. *Wedgwood cameo.*

AESCULAPIUS AND HYGEIA

The use of a figure called *Aesculapius* or *Moses* was very popular in Wedgwood ware. It is that of an old man, carrying a serpent-entwined staff, whose hair streams off his face. There is an example in the Winthrop Bequest, no. 11; [25] no. 151 in the *Sale Catalogue of Beautiful Old Wedgwood Belonging to Horace Townsend* is another. Raspe [26] lists and illustrates a rock crystal in which this figure of Aesculapius tallies exactly with that in the Wedgwood cameo. It is a Renaissance gem modelled by Valerio Vicentino. In view of the various inaccuracies of the Wedgwood *Catalogues*, caused not a little by the fact that the potter secured some of his designs second-hand, that is, from Tassie, it is quite possible that this figure is derived from the rock crystal and not from an un-identified carnelian which is the source given in the *Catalogue*.[27]

The companion figure on this gem, called *Hygeia* or *Peace*, is that of a clothed female holding out an olive branch in her right hand. In Wedgwood this is often made into a separate cameo, as no. 12 in the *Winthrop Bequest Catalogue*, where it is listed under the name Hygeia. Meteyard, in *Choice Examples of Wedgwood Art*, Pl. XVI, illustrates a frame of cameos, one of which is the complete gem of *Aesculapius and Hygeia*. Plate 12. Hygeia holds a

Plate 13. Aesculapius and Hygeia. *Wedgwood plaque.*

snake in her left hand in addition to the branch in her right. An altar, a tree, and a pedestal topped by a lamp appear between the two figures. Meteyard also states that most of the cameos in this frame were derived from Tassie paste impressions. A Tassie impression of the crystal exists in the Boggs Collection in the Walters Art Gallery, Baltimore, drawer T, no. 1113.

Another use of two figures named Aesculapius and Hygeia is illustrated in Meteyard, *Choice Examples of Wedgwood Art,* Pl. III. "Bas-relief or tablet. Blue jasper, white relief. Height 8¼ inches; width 6⅞ inches. This exquisite piece is taken from a bas-relief [28] in the Capitoline Museum, Rome. Pacetti . . . made a model in wax early in 1788 . . ." In the original Greek marble relief, Aesculapius sits on a cushioned chair with a curved back and leans his right arm over the back of it. Hygeia, her feet crossed and swathed in a himation, leans her right elbow on a pedestal. A snake is curled at her feet. In the background are two pilasters; from the right one is hung one end of a swag of drapery. The relief is Greek in subject and in composition. The elegant proportions and somewhat affected pose of Hygeia are later, however, and suggest a good Roman copy.[29] The jasper relief, Plate 13, is a most exact reproduction of the marble one.

Plate 14. Apollo. *Wedgwood cameo.*

APOLLO

Among the many representations of Apollo used by Wedgwood, three definitely derived from the antique stand out.

The first to be discussed is illustrated in Meteyard, *Life of Josiah Wedgwood,* II, p. 148, Fig. 32. She says of it on page 140, "The Body used for the Etruscan vases . . . was the black basalts, . . . On this, groups, figures, were painted chiefly in red." The example discussed is in the Victoria and Albert Museum. The origin of this design is Plate 84, Volume I, of d'Hancarville's *Antiquities* in the cabinet of Sir William Hamilton, 1766 edition, and is called *Apollo chasing Daphne.* It is a lost vase, and the shape is unknown though it is thought to be the style of the "Shuvalov" painter.[30]

The second, Plate 14, in Rathbone, *Old Wedgwood,* Pl. LI, derives from an amethyst [31] in the Treasury of St. Denis. Apollo leans on his lyre on a pedestal, and on his other side is a tripod on another pedestal. As it appears in the Raspe catalogue, it might have come to Wedgwood through a Tassie impression.

The third, *Apollo, Diomedes, and Aeneas,* is a pottery gem in the collection of the author. Light blue jasper, white relief. Story-

Maskelyne [32] identifies the subject on the original gem as Apollo coming between Diomed and Aeneas, thereby allowing Aeneas to escape into the city of Troy; Furtwängler,[33] not so convincingly, calls it Patroclus and Apollo. It is an intaglio showing Apollo between Diomed, who is striking at a cloud unrepresented in the gem, and Aeneas, who is seen disappearing into the city through a gate. The original gem has been variously described as a sard,[34] carnelian,[35] and beryl.[36] It has been in the possession of Caylus,[37] and Lord Bessborough,[38] and finally came into the Marlborough collection.[39] Furtwängler considers it to be of Augustan workmanship, but Story-Maskelyne doubts the antiquity of this work. Wedgwood might have worked from the original, as the Marlborough collection was known to have been opened to him. In the pottery version a small obelisk and vase have been added to the left field of the composition. There is a cast of the original gem in the Thomas A. Bogg Collection of Tassie Impressions, drawer FF, no. 1745, Raspe, no. 9381, II, p. 548.

Plate 15. Heracles in the Garden of the Hesperides. *Wedgwood plaque.*

ATHENIAN TRIBAL HEROES

On one of the first vases thrown at Etruria, illustrated in Meteyard, *Life of Josiah Wedgwood,* II, p. 113, was a so-called "Etruscan" urn; one, that is, painted on black basalts in direct imitation of the ancient glazed Greek pots. The design was taken from part of one of the Hamilton vases [40] now in the British Museum. It is a hydria in the later fine style [41] and is known as the Meidias hydria, one of the best known vases of antiquity. The design consists merely of several male figures grouped in various attitudes. On the ancient vase there was a woman at each end of the group. Also taken from the same vase is the composition known as "Heracles in the Garden of the Hesperides," [42] Plate 15, illustrated in jasper in Barnard, *Chats on Wedgwood Ware,* p. 130. It was modelled for Wedgwood by Flaxman.

Both designs are taken from the lower frieze of the vase.

Plate 16. Cassandra grasping the Palladium. *Wedgwood plaque.*

CASSANDRA GRASPING THE PALLADIUM
Plate 16

Illustrated in Meteyard, *Memorials of Wedgwood,* Pl. XXVI, no. 1, this stands no. 33 in Class II of the French *Catalogue* of 1788, in which it is described as "belle figure en basse, tirée d'une gemme du cabinet du Roi de France." This gem [43] does not tally with the pottery bas-relief. The figure of Cassandra is the same: she is half-nude, rests on one knee, and clasps a statue, her head thrown back, her hair streaming down her back. But there is, on the gem, a statue of Priapus, and the knee of the Cassandra figure rests on a prow-shaped object in which sits a figure drinking from a wine cup. The statue which she holds is a female blowing the double flute. These accessories give a Dionysiac air and identify the figure as a maenad, not a Cassandra. In the Wedgwood medallion, Cassandra is fundamentally the same figure, but she rests her knee on a square cippus, decorated at the corners with rams' heads, which are connected by garlands. She grasps a helmeted female figure, and to the right is the bust of a bearded man on a high pedestal which has, one-third up, a scroll-like decorative motif. This Wedgwood relief corresponds in every detail with an ancient bas-relief [44] now in the Louvre.[45] The statue which Cassandra holds, the cippus and its decoration, the draped bust of the bearded philosopher, and even the little scrolls on the pedestal are all exactly the same. Wedgwood definitely gives the source, yet it is not the correct one. This could be an uncatalogued relief, but it is more likely an error since the main figures in the ancient bas-relief and the eighteenth-century pottery relief are so much alike.

Plate 17. The Crowning of a Citharist or the Apotheosis of Homer.
Wedgwood vase.

THE CROWNING OF A CITHARIST
OR THE APOTHEOSIS OF HOMER
Plate 17

Illustrated in Meteyard, *Wedgwood and His Works,* Pl. II. Bas-relief or tablet. "Designed by Flaxman for Wedgwood between 1777 and 1779. It appeared subsequently in various forms and sizes." It is listed as no. 202, in Class II in the French Catalogue of 1788. Elsewhere [46] Meteyard also says of this design, "It has been questioned whether the *Apotheosis of Homer* as that also of Virgil, are Flaxman's work, but a reference to the former . . . will . . . confirm the generally received opinion that both were modelled by him." Constable [47] upholds Meteyard in this statement. Meteyard says the original of this design is a print or model of a "bas-relief which at that date formed part of the collection in the Colonna Palace, Rome." [48] It is accepted that the original design for this piece is a bell crater [49] of the finest period, once in the Hamilton collection and now in the British Museum. The main design depicts a citharist victorious. In the center, a bearded man carrying a cithara puts one foot on a base of two steps. A nike flies toward him from the left, while on the right another nike stands with hand outstretched. There are two seated figures, that of a bearded man to the right and that of a female figure with a spear to the left. Wedgwood has adapted the design so faithfully that there is no doubt or difficulty in identifying the source of the design.

Plate 18. Demeter searching for Persephone. *Wedgwood cameo.*

DEMETER SEARCHING FOR PERSEPHONE

Illustrated in Meteyard, *Wedgwood and His Works,* Pl. XV, bottom pottery cameo in frame 2. This jasper gem, Plate 18, derives from one in the collection of the King of France.[50] The goddess strides to the left carrying in her right hand a torch, in her left a scythe. At her feet on the original emerald are two serpents which Wedgwood has omitted and for which he has substituted a feathery bush. This probably came to the potter through Tassie as it is no. 1853 in Raspe, I, p. 140. This figure was also used by Adam in the ceiling of the drawing room at Syon House, Middlesex, 1761–1768.[51]

Plate 19. Diomedes and the Palladium. *Wedgwood medallion.*

DIOMEDES AND THE PALLADIUM
Plate 19

Illustrated in Meteyard, *Memorials of Wedgwood*, Pl. VI. "Of this small bas-relief, Wedgwood has several copies; the last made, just prior to 1777, being probably a fresh model from the hand of Flaxman. The original gem—like the Marriage of Cupid and Psyche —is still in the Marlborough Collection. It is the work of Dioscorides, one of the most celebrated gem engravers of the Augustan age. The subject is an important event in the Trojan war—the seizing and carrying off of the Palladium, or guardian deity, of Troy. Diomedes appears descending from a square altar, holding in his left hand the Palladium, and in his right a sword. The guardian lies dead at his feet, and the statue of Minerva upon a cippus turns her back to him that she may not witness the bloody sacrilege. . . . In Tassie's catalogue are seventy-eight gems which represent this subject, yet the list is not complete." Illustrated also is no. 26 of the Winthrop Bequest of Old Wedgwood in the Fogg Museum. Meteyard's comments quoted above may also be applied to this piece.

No. 27 of the Winthrop Bequest bears the name Gnaios in Greek, and the original gem [52] can be definitely identified as a sardonyx in the possession of the Duke of Devonshire. It should be noted here that the Dioscorides gem, a carnelian, which Meteyard suggests as the source of her illustration, was not in the Marlborough but in the Devonshire Collection,[53] and the figure with its back turned is identified as Poseidon. There is an interesting difference in drapery arrangement between no. 26 of the Winthrop Bequest and the relief illustrated in Meteyard. In the Winthrop Diomedes, the chlamys of the hero falls in front of him; whereas in the Meteyard illustration it falls in back of him, as it does on both the Devonshire gems of the subject. As no. 26 of the Winthrop Bequest is dated 1792, it is probable that the new arrangement of the drapery to offset the complete nakedness of the hero is the result of the anti-nudity campaign mentioned in a letter to Flaxman in 1790. It is interesting to note in the study of this particular representation of *Diomedes and the Palladium* that there is no mention of the luna marble relief [54] in the Naples Museum which is called *Orestes in Delphi* [55] and which is a copy of an original Greek relief. The composition is almost the same as that of the gems; a nude young man grasping a sword in one hand rises from a square base, which is also decorated with a spray of leaves. There is also the statue with its back to the hero and a sleeping figure at its base. There is no statue in his left hand as there is in the gems. The original of the Naples relief, or even the Naples relief itself, might have served as model for the gems as it is well known that great works of art were reproduced on gems in ancient as well as modern times.

Plate 20. Birth of Dionysus. *Wedgwood plaque.*

DIONYSUS (BACCHUS)

It was the worship of this god more than that of any other god, which retained the character of orgiastic nature-worship in ancient times. The early Greek world represented this god of nature by a phallic herm. From this was developed the stately form of the old bearded Dionysus, and in the time of Praxiteles the youthful Dionysus was conceived.[56] His companions are satyrs; drunken Sileni; Pans; dancing, often furious, females called maenads; and centaurs. Born prematurely of Semele, he was set in the thigh of Zeus. Immediately after his birth, Hermes carried him to Mount Nysa, where the nymphs and satyrs reared him. He later took as his bride Ariadne, and rode in a bridal chariot with her to Olympus. He is often represented as surrounded by maenads, punishing Pentheus and Lycurgus, the insulters of his worship, and also the Tyrrhenian pirates. Bacchus is the Latin form of this god's name and is more commonly used in the eighteenth century; he is, however, referred to as Dionysus as far as possible in the following discussion.

In *Birth of Dionysus,* Hermes delivers the baby god to the nymphs of Nysa. This Wedgwood version, Plate 20, was inspired by the marble vase [57] signed by Salpion,[58] an Athenian sculptor of

unknown date. The Parian marble vase was found at Cormia on
the gulf of Gaeta and was used as a font in the Cathedral of Gaeta
but was afterwards removed to the museum in Naples. A Wedgwood copy, now in the museum at Etruria, is illustrated in
Barnard, *Chats on Wedgwood Ware,* p. 168. Wedgwood mentions
in a letter to Bentley, Jan. 6, 1776, a *Birth and Triumph of Bacchus* as done by Hackwood, ". . . Hackwood has nearly finished
the two tablets of the *Birth and Triumph of Bacchus,* but am
afraid we shall not be able to make either of them in a continued
tablet . . . we could make them to fill a frieze very cleverly in
separate pieces . . ." Besides the plaque now in the Etruria
Museum, there is an illustration in Pl. XI, no. 2, Meteyard, *Wedgwood and His Works,* of three Bacchanalian figures, two of which
appear in the above-mentioned Scene on Mount Nysa. Therefore,
this is probably the Triumph in "separate" pieces of 1776. There
are two *Birth of Bacchus* tablets mentioned in the French *Catalogue* of 1788, Class II, no. 1 and no. 118, which is described as
"après l'antique." As the source for this scene is no doubt the
marble vase, it may be assumed that no. 118 is exemplified by the
plaque in the Etruria Museum. In this particular case the design
is not translated literally into pottery. This is much in the nature
of an adaptation. The central group of Hermes, child, and seated
nymph is fundamentally unchanged except for the addition of
wings to the cap of Hermes and a general baby-doll look to the
faces and figures of the principals. It is in the attendants that there
is found a great difference. The end figure, while in the same position, no longer leans against a tree with her upstretched arm but
carries a cup. The second figure from the right remains exactly
the same, completely clothed and carrying a thyrsus. The third
figure, instead of being a semidraped, bearded old man leaning
on his thyrsus, is a completely nude youth blowing a horn. The
three figures to the left of the central group have been exchanged
for one figure of an almost completely nude youth carrying a large
vase. It is hard to suggest a reason for this change. The substitu-
tions certainly constitute no improvement over the original, which
is a late and graceful Hellenistic work.

In the group of *Three Bacchanalian Figures,* the two end ones are from the group described above, the woman with the cup and the youth with the vase. The center is a half-draped male with vine leaves on his head, one hand raised above his head. It has been adapted from a Plate in Montfaucon.[59] Artistically, these two groups are not successful. They exemplify too well the eighteenth-century concept of classic art in the extreme grace, prettiness and slickness of their execution. They certainly lack the character and dignity of the ancient work of art.

Plate 21. Birth of Bacchus from "Cachet of Michelangelo."
Wedgwood plaque.

There is another version of the *Birth of Dionysus,* Plate 21, called in the Catalogue of 1788, *Birth of Bacchus.* Bas-relief or tablet; blue jasper; white relief; length 20½ inches, height 9½ inches. Illustrated in Meteyard, *Choice Examples of Wedgwood Art,* Pl. XII. It is modelled from the so-called "Cachet of Michelangelo" in the cabinet of the King of France.[60] It is no. 216 in Class I, section I (intaglios), and no. 216 in Class II (bas-reliefs, medallions, tablets). It is called the "Cachet of Michelangelo" not because it is supposed to have been executed by him but because it is supposed to have been owned by him. It is a carnelian and represents a lively vintage scene. As Dionysus and the vine are closely allied, its use as a celebration of the birth of the god is not too farfetched.

Plate 22. Education of Dionysus. *Wedgwood plaque.*

Education of Dionysus, Plate 22. Illustrated in Meteyard, *Wedgwood and His Works,* Pl. III, no. 1. Bas-relief or tablet; pale blue jasper; white relief; 11¼ inches by 6¾ inches. "It appears to be an adapted portion of a larger plaque; the woman on the right being evidently one of a group which balanced the fine one to the left." Meteyard is correct in the surmise above, for the design is taken from one half the side of a sarcophagus in the Galleria of the Capitoline Museum, Plate 23.[61] The sarcophagus was brought in 1740 from the church of San Biagio at Nepi and presented by Benedict XIV to the museum. The composition is well

Plate 23. Education of Dionysus. *Source.*

designed: the figures are graceful and lively; the whole is emi-
nently Greek in feeling and recalls the late fourth century and
early Hellenistic types.[62] The part utilized in the Wedgwood
plaque represents the child Dionysus standing on a rock attended
by nymphs and satyrs. To the right of this group is a young satyr
holding up a cup, while Silenus beats another satyr crouched before a skin of wine. The tablet cuts off the rest of the sarcophagal
design except for one nymph who on the original clashes cymbals,
and the barest suggestion of another nymph who on the original is
seated and holds the infant god. It is an odd adaptation of an
antique work, for without the two parts of nymphs included, the
two scenes represented would have supplied sufficient subject mat-

Plate 24. Apollo instructing the youthful Dionysus. *Wedgwood plaque.*

ter. As it is, the composition is unsatisfactory though those parts
used are completely true to the ancient source.

What is in the Wedgwood called "Apollo instructing the Youthful Bacchus (Dionysus)," Plate 24, is really of unknown subject
matter. It has been called "Bacchic Scene," [63] or "Alcibiades among
the Courtesans," [64] or "Apollo and the Three Graces." [65] Illustrated in Meteyard, *Wedgwood and His Works*, Pl. V, no. 2. Bas-
relief or tablet. Light blue jasper; white relief; 15 inches by 6½
inches. "A composition piece of probably early date." In it, the
central figure, which shall be here identified as Dionysus, holds a
lyre in his left hand and touches the cymbals held by a bacchante
who leans her head on his shoulder. There are two almost nude

female figures on a couch to the left of the main figure. A semidraped female leaning on a pedestal has been added to the left
field of the Wedgwood adaptation. The original marble relief is in
the Naples museum and is a Roman copy of a Hellenistic work.[66]

Dionysus and Panther, Plate 25. Illustrated in Meteyard, *Memorials of Josiah Wedgwood,* Pl. VII. It is also illustrated in black

Plate 25. Dionysus and Panther. *Wedgwood plaque.*

basalt in Barnard, *op. cit.,* p. 169; Maurice H. Grant, *Makers of
Black Basaltes,* Pl. L, no. 3. Oval medallion; 13½ inches high;
ground and frame black; relief white biscuit. "Modelled from a
bas-relief taken from the Monument of Lysicrates at Athens. The
first medallion seems to have been made in November, 1772, for
Sir W. W. Wynne . . . Choicest examples of this medallion are
in blue and white jasper." The original frieze has suffered greatly
in the nineteenth century, but there is a cast of it in the British
Museum executed for Lord Elgin. The subject of the frieze is the
victory of Dionysus over the Tyrrhenian pirates who had made
him prisoner at Chios with the intention of selling him as a slave.
The god revenged himself by transforming his attackers into
dolphins. This particular medallion represents the god resting
with his panther.[67] It is quite possible that Wedgwood received
the idea for this design from his friend James Stuart, coauthor with

Revett of *Antiquities of Athens,* the first volume of which appeared in 1762, although the entire frieze from the Monument of Lysicrates was used by Robert Adam on the Great Portico, Stowe [68] in Buckinghamshire, 1771.

The tablet called "Bacchanalian Triumph," Plate 26, as well as vases, candelabra, smaller tablets, a Muse type, and one of the figures from the *Dancing Hours* derive their motifs and forms from the Borghese Vase [69] now in the Salle des Caryatides of the Louvre.

Plate 26. Bacchanalian Triumph. *Wedgwood plaque.*

It is a large vase of Pentelic marble found where the Gardens of Sallust used to be.[70] The figures, excellently carved in bas-relief, represent a Dionysiac ceremony. The elegance and grace of the group evidently captivated Wedgwood as he used the figures over and over as a whole and separately but always exactly as they were on the original vase.

Centaur and Young Dionysus. Illustrated in Meteyard, *Life of Josiah Wedgwood,* II, p. 360. 16 inches in diameter; black basalts. Although it is called "Centaur and Young Achilles," the thyrsus carried by the centaur seems to identify the youth definitely as Dionysus. This is no doubt one of the Herculaneum figures classed under *Centaurs,* in the *Catalogue* of 1788, nos. 57–59 in Class II. Meteyard does not identify it as such, merely listing it as one of the eighty-two tablets appearing in the first edition of the *Catalogue.* The original wall painting from the House of Cicero in Pompeii [71] has been reproduced quite faithfully, in every twist of drapery and even to the tying of the bow at the top of the thyrsus. However, the figures in the Wedgwood seem rounder and the young Dionysus is a chubby youth.

Plate 27. Endymion on Latmos. *Source.*

ENDYMION ON LATMOS
Frontispiece and Plate 27

Illustrated in Rathbone, *Old Wedgwood,* Pl. II. It is supposed to have been modelled by Pacetti in 1789 from the famous bas-relief [72] in the Capitoline Museum. Endymion is seated asleep on a rock; his head droops, and a spear rests on his left shoulder. His dog is above him, head raised and obviously barking. This marble relief of Endymion is unique and has no likeness to any other representation or painting of the myth. It has been dated from the Flavian period.[73] There is also a gem in Raspe's *Catalogue*

Raisonné, no. 2162, Pl. XXIX, signed by Marchant, and still another gem bearing exactly the same design belonging to Lord Montagu illustrated in Worlidge, *Select Collection of Drawings from Curious Antique Gems,* no. 171. It was evidently a most popular subject in the eighteenth century by the time that Wedgwood reproduced it in pottery.

EROS OR CUPID

There are so many examples of the use of *erotes* in Wedgwood ware that only those instances in which the sources are definitely identified are discussed. Use of *putti, amorini, erotes,* or cupids was revived in the Renaissance and reached its height in the time of the Rococo. In ancient art the concept of Eros changed from time to time. In archaic Greek art, figures of Eros were rare; in the fifth century B.C. he was a young man; in the fourth century the Eros type of Praxiteles became the model for many statues. The Praxitelean Eros was a winged youth endowed with almost feminine grace, whose coiffeur is curly and short or long and elegantly curled. The Alexandrian poets pictured him as an infant, mischievous and malicious. His attributes are usually wings, bow and arrows, and torches. He appears in art associated with his mother Aphrodite, his bride Psyche, and Dionysus.

Erotes in Hellenistic art lose their mythological meaning and are used as a means of expressing shades of emotion. They are now a race of little winged genies who are present in almost all the mythological and hero cycles. They are particularly numerous in the wall paintings of Pompeii, in which they can be seen in all the occupations of daily life, fishing, garland-making, wine-making. Roman art followed the Alexandrian tradition, and *erotes* appear even on funerary monuments in the various occupations. It is at this time that Eros becomes the genius of the dead and is represented as serious and preoccupied, often leaning on a torch, or asleep. In this aspect he is connected closely with Psyche, the symbol of the soul.

Marriage of Cupid and Psyche, Plate 28. Illustrated in Meteyard, *Life of Josiah Wedgwood,* II, p. 358. Miss Meteyard states, *Life,* II, p. 357 ff., "Amongst the number [of gems] are some of the finest subjects of antique art as interpreted by the gem engravers of the Alexandrian school and later of the Augustine age. At the close of the earliest list of cameos we have the 'Marriage of Cupid and Psyche'; this was first obtained from a sulphur cast by Tassie, but afterwards freshly modelled from the original gem and given to the world in both fine biscuit and uncoloured jasper with blue grounds and in sizes from the largest oval plaque to the minutest ring gem for a lady's finger. . . . Its original may well be called one of the finest specimens of ancient art. . . ." In reality, as Miss Meteyard admits in a later work, *Choice Example of Wedgwood*

Plate 28. Marriage of Cupid and Psyche. *Wedgwood medallion.*

Art, Pl. I, the original gem,[74] a sardonyx with figures in a coffee hue, once in the Arundel Collection, then in the Marlborough Collection, and now in the Museum of Fine Arts, Boston, has been identified as a Renaissance product.[75] Story-Maskelyne says of it,[76] "In point of technique it has never been surpassed in any age." The introduction of the dove, the veiling of the bride, the use of the cord to unite the two, and lastly the confinement of the composition between two horizontal lines as well as the lettering of the signature condemn the stone [77] as an antique. It is easy to see that this would be popular since its sweetness and delicacy as well as its actual subject matter have appealed to the general public and will continue to do so. The fact that it was made in all sizes, colors, and materials speaks for the immense sale it must have seen.

Sale of Erotes. Illustrated in Meteyard, *Choice Examples of*

Wedgwood Art, Pl. XVI. Meteyard states that the subjects of these
pottery cameos were chiefly taken from the Tassie pastes, but the
source is a wall painting [78] from Stabia now in the museum at
Naples, Plate 29. Many allegorical meanings have been read into
this charming colored mural. It represents a seated woman lifting
an eros out of a cage by its wings and offering it to two other

Plate 29. Sale of Erotes. *Source.*

women, one seated, in the left ground of the painting. Rathbone,
Catalogue of the Wedgwood Museum, p. 70, has stated that the
original was a work by a Frenchman, Constant. Gorely, *Old Wedgwood,* 1941, p. 75, points out that Constant was a French modeller
who had also executed the subject, but in white biscuit, that Rathbone saw this and assumed that it had served as a model for Wedgwood. However, the subject had gained wide notoriety in France,
and it has been described as "artistically the revolutionary bomb-
shell of the eighteenth century." [79] The artist, Vien, painted it in
1763, and it hangs in the Palace at Fontainebleau. 1763 was five
years before the founding of the factory at Etruria and about fif-

teen years before the invention of jasper ware. The fact that it was a well-known subject is shown by its use in interior decoration in many of the palaces decorated at that time, one of them being the palace of Catherine II at Tsarskoe-Seloe.[80] Another example of its popularity is the eighteenth-century gem, signed by Cades,[81] that was inspired by the painting; in this, the seller of *erotes* is derived exactly from the mural, but she offers her wares to a nude female.

Plate 30. Psyche Wounded and Bound by Cupids. *Wedgwood medallion.*

It could have been no novelty to the artistic world, and there was no doubt a ready market for this subject which has been accredited with starting a new art epoch.

Psyche Wounded and Bound by Cupids, Plate 30. Illustrated in Meteyard, *Wedgwood and His Works,* Pl. XIII. "Oval plaque or medallion. Dark blue jasper, white relief. Height $2\frac{3}{4}$ inches, length $4\frac{1}{4}$ inches. . . . Probably a somewhat late but beautiful medallion." It is known that Wedgwood possessed a copy of the Comte de Caylus' "Recueil." In Volume II, Plate LXXXVI, no. 3, is part of a design from a vase carrying this subject matter. At first glance this would seem to be the source. Two of Wedgwood's other source books,[82] however, have an engraving from a gem that, it can be safely said, is the derivation of the fundamental figure design. Psyche, half-nude, and wearing wings that are not butterfly wings but shield-shaped, is bound to a tree. One eros ties her while the other beats her. On the original gem, there is a fourth figure of a seated woman to the right. She is omitted in the

Plate 31. Venus and Cupid. *Wedgwood medallion.*

Wedgwood version. Several small changes take place in the translation of the design into pottery. Psyche is now completely draped as are the two *erotes;* her wings are changed to butterfly wings, and other little trees and plants are added to the field. There is as usual a softness and sweetness present in the eighteenth-century version that was not in the original.

Eros on Lion. Illustrated in Meteyard, *Wedgwood and His Works,* Pl. XVI, one of a frame of nine cameos. The source of design is probably the sardonyx [83] in the Medici Collection. Wedgwood has not only added a tree but wrapped the tail, which is curved in the original, between the legs of the lion, supposedly to portray better the submission of the lion to the lyre-playing of the god.

Aphrodite carrying flower of fertility, preceded by an eros, called "Venus and Cupid," Plate 31. Illustrated in Meteyard,

Memorials of Wedgwood, Pl. IV, and by a jasper relief, no. 03.277, in the Museum of Fine Arts, Boston. One of nine basalt intaglios; 2½ inches high. The source is a carnelian gem.[84] Aphrodite strides to the side, her draperies billowing out behind her. In one hand she carries a spray, two leaves of which are erect and two flowers

Plate 32. Selene and Eros, Selene visiting Endymion. *Source.*

Plate 33. Selene and Eros, Selene visiting Endymion. *Wedgwood plaque.*

of which hang. The little eros who precedes Aphrodite reaches up for the blossoms. This is an exact adaptation and was probably derived from one of the prints in the source books of Wedgwood as it appears in three of them. Of great interest is the use of this motif by the architects and interior decorators Robert and James Adam as an inset on the frame of a pier glass dating 1762–1765 for the Earl of Bute.[85]

Selene and Eros, also called *Venus and Cupid,* Plates 32 and 33. Illustrated in Meteyard, *Memorials of Wedgwood,* Pl. IV. This bas-relief group seems to have been taken from the Sarcophagus of Gerontia [86] now in the Stanza del Fauno in the Capitoline Museum. It is Selene wearing her usual costume, a long chiton, crescent on her head and himation flowing crescentwise behind

Plate 34. Offering to Peace. *Wedgwood plaque.*

her. Eros carrying a small torch precedes her. In the basalt intaglio Eros does not carry the torch although his hand is in the same position as when he did, and he has been draped. There is one example of the use of the entire sarcophagal design on jasper in Rathbone, *Old Wedgwood*, Pl. XXXIII, in the Tweedmouth Collection. It is called in Wedgwood *Diana visiting Endymion*

Plate 35. So-called "Sacrifice to Hymen." *Wedgwood plaque.*

and reproduces the subject matter faithfully. Endymion is asleep in the lap of an old bearded man, Hypnos; Selene and Eros approach him from the right. In the background is a small reclining figure on a rocky elevation representing Mt. Latmos. To the right is the chariot of the goddess attended by two more *erotes*.

It is interesting to note that while there is only one complete copy of the sarcophagus, these two figures of Selene and Eros are used over and over again, in basalt and jasper, and often appear in other compositions combined with figures from other sources. An example of this is the appearance of the goddess and her little companion in a composition piece called *Offering to Peace,* Plate 34, illustrated in Meteyard, *Memorials of Wedgwood,* Pl. XXIII, no. 3. They are the third figure group from the left. In many cases the torch of Eros and the crescent of Selene are omitted.

Plate 36. So-called "Sacrifice to Hymen." *Source.*

The so-called "Sacrifice to Hymen," Plates 35 and 36. Illustrated in Meteyard, *Memorials of Wedgwood,* Pl. XXII. Jasper; pale blue and white; 10½ inches by 5¼ inches. Attributed to Flaxman by Meteyard, but "there is uncertainty on the point." It consists of a series of small *erotes* playing instruments, carrying torches, and dancing. It was copied from the cinerary urn of D. Lucullus Felix,[87] now in the Galleria of the Capitoline Museum. The Wedgwood version might well be a product of the atelier in Rome over which Flaxman presided. The urn is octagonal. At all upper angles are bearded masks connected by wreaths and loops. On each side except one bearing an inscription, in high relief, is the figure of an eros. The series represents a miniature thiasos, a symbol of the hope of life after death. It is a fresh and dainty work of the early empire. Supposed to have been found in a tomb on the Via Appia, it was formerly in the Cesi and Albani Collections.[88] Its appeal would be the same as that of the *Cupid and Psyche* subject matter, that is, small rounded cherubs performing adult acts, and it no doubt saw great sale.

Eros and the Infant Hermes, called "Cupid and the Infant

Plate 37. Eros and the Infant Hermes. *Source.*

Mercury," Plates 37 and 38. Illustrated in Meteyard, *Memorials of Wedgwood,* Pl. XIII. "Ornamental vase on plinth. Jasper, pink ground, white relief; height 10⅝ inches by 5½ inches. . . . A chariot is drawn by rams, on one of which Cupid is seated as driver, whilst Mercury stands at the foot. The chariot is filled with the caduceus, a helmet, and a vase. This bas-relief appears to

Plate 38. Eros and the Infant Hermes. *Wedgwood plaque.*

have been copied from an intaglio, and this from a paste by Tassie." It is not to a gem that we must look for the source of this relief but rather to a sarcophagus [89] now in the Stanza del Fauno in the Capitoline Museum. The sarcophagus is of luna marble and bears a relief of *erotes* as charioteers each carrying the attributes of a different deity. The Wedgwood relief is taken from the first chariot on the left. The scene as a whole represents a playful variation on the triumph of Dionysus.[90] It is here suggested that this too was a product of the school at Rome working for Wedgwood.

Plate 39. Flora. *Source*.

Plate 40. Flora. *Figure from a Wedgwood vase.*

FLORA

Plates 39 and 40

Illustrated by pottery vase, no. 96.831 in Museum of Fine Arts, Boston. Called "Venus" or "Ceres" in the *Catalogue of Old Wedgwood in the . . . Winthrop Bequest,* Fogg Museum, no. 14, in which it is described, "Full length draped figure holding floral wreath in right hand to shoulder and drapery in left. . . . Modelled from a carnelian (*Wedgwood Catalogue,* 1787). . . ." Notwithstanding the assignment of the source, even by Wedgwood himself, to a carnelian, it is evident that the original of the figure whether through a gem or print is the so-called Farnese Flora [91] (Plate 39) in the museum at Naples. In most details they tally. Her chiton slips off her right shoulder and is arranged in a cascade of drapery on the left side. She is girt about her hips, and the chiton is bloused slightly over the encircling band. She stands in a slightly hip-shot and very graceful position, holding her skirt in her right hand. The difference between the original and the Wedgwood version resolves itself down to the question of the restoration of the hand bearing the wreath in the pottery and a branch in the statue. Since the statue itself is restored, any variation of an adaptation would be equally valid. In most seventeenth- and eighteenth-century prints the Flora bears the wreath.[92]

Plate 41. Friendship Consoling Affliction. *Wedgwood medallion.*

FRIENDSHIP CONSOLING AFFLICTION

Plate 41

Illustrated in Meteyard, *Wedgwood and His Works,* Pl XIII, no. 3. "Bas-relief or medallion. Long oval. 4¾ inches by 3 inches. Dark blue jasper; white relief . . . From a design by Lady Templetown." It is no. 240, Class II, in the French *Catalogue* of 1788. In reading about artists who "created" designs for Wedgwood, one usually finds the name of Lady Templeto(w)n. In this case, however, her design has been copied (for it is too close to the original to use the term "inspired") from an antique bas-relief [93] once in the Palazzo Albani and now in the Louvre. It is called "The New Bride." Not only do the general attitudes of the figures match, but even the details of coiffure, the background swags and falls of drapery are identical. In the original, the weeping bride has her feet sponged by the attendant; in the pottery version, the attending female pours liquid over the feet of the bride. That is the extent of the "adaptation." It is also most interesting to note the use of this same relief in a panel over a chimney piece in the library [94] of Syon House, seat of the Duke of Northumberland in Middlesex, which dates 1761–1769, and also under the dome of the Reges House [95] in Edinburgh, which dates from 1771 on. Both edifices were designed by the Adam brothers. The title "Friend-ship Consoling Affliction" is a sop, one supposes, to the moralizing tendencies of the eighteenth-century English. As a whole, it is a most pleasant little relief.

Plate 42. Ganymede and the Eagle. *Wedgwood medallion.*

GANYMEDE AND THE EAGLE

Plates 42 and 43

Illustrated in Meteyard, *Wedgwood and His Works,* Pl. X, no. 3.
Oval medallion. Light blue jasper; white relief; 7½ inches by 5¼
inches. "This exquisite gem was modelled at Etruria between
1777 and 1779. It stands no. 225 in the fifth edition of the *Catalogue.* Wedgwood thus refers to this bas-relief in a letter to Bentley, April 14, 1778: 'We shall send you three pieces of jasper today
from Sir Roger Newdigate's models, which with the Eagle and

Plate 43. Ganymede and the Eagle. *Source.*

Ganymede should be sent with our compliments.' " This subject is no. 31 in the *Catalogue of Old Wedgwood from the . . . Winthrop Bequest* in the Fogg Museum. It is said of it and its source, "Design from a Roman sardonyx in the collection of the Duke of Marlborough (Choix de Pierres Antiques Gravées du Cabinet du Duc de Marlborough, Vol. II, Pl. XLIII), also initial letter in d'Hancarville's Catalogue of Sir Wm. Hamilton's collection, p. 36." This, however, may be a different version of "Ganymede" than is illustrated in Meteyard. It seems that the source of the Meteyard "Ganymede" is the picture of a relief illustrated in Bartoli and Bellori, *Veterum Sepulcra*, Pl. CX. There are certain similarities of drapery, position, and figure style that declare source and copy. The Ganymede of the Wedgwood relief is a nude, well-developed muscular youth who wears a band around his head and whose drapery spills over his seat and lap. He holds a goblet out of which the eagle drinks. Both boy and eagle as well as the folds of drapery compare closely with the illustration. An early nineteenth-century gem after this same source can be seen in Lippold, *Gemmen,* Pl. CXXXVIII, no. 4, signed by Von Frey.

Plate 44. Three Graces. *Wedgwood cameo.*

GRACES

Three Graces, Plate 44. Illustrated in Meteyard, *Wedgwood and His Works,* Pl. XVI, a frame of nine cameos. Two cameos derive from the relief on a fourth-century lecythus [96] of Athenian style now in the British Museum and illustrated in d'Hancarville [97] who calls the subject matter unknown. There are three Charites (?) in relief with hair knotted up; the center one is nude although sometimes draped in the Wedgwood; the other two wear long girt chitons. The one on the left has a vase in the right hand and a basket of fruit in the left. The basket of fruit is not apparent in either the d'Hancarville print or the cameo. The one on the right has a himation over her left arm. A Wedgwood medallion of this subject is no. 21 in the *Catalogue of Old Wedgwood from the Bequest of Grenville Lindall Winthrop,* now in the Fogg Museum of Art, Cambridge, Massachusetts, in which the source is described as follows, "Design from a carnelian in the collection of the King of Naples (*Wedgwood Catalogue,* 1787); also in d'Hancarville's Catalogue of Sir William Hamilton's Collection, Vol. II, Pl. 94. Note that the artist has draped the center figure." There is a gem signed by (G.) Pichler of this subject,[98] which is no. 6443 in Raspe's *Catalogue Raisonné.* This was not in the collection of the King of Naples but belonged to Prince Poniatowski and was not a carnelian but chalcedony gem. Since Wedgwood's catalogue mentions "Three Graces" from a carnelian belonging to the King of Naples, it is no doubt referring to no. 6436 in Raspe, which is a different figure grouping of the same subject. In the Boggs Collection, drawer F, no. 306 is a cast of the subject under discussion. Meteyard in *Choice Examples of Wedgwood Art,* Pl. XVI, illustrates a frame of twenty-two cameos, one of which is this subject, *The Three Graces,* with the center figure nude. She states in her discussion of these cameos, "The subjects are chiefly taken from Tassie's pastes . . ." It is also known that the potter worked from original vases in the collection of Sir William Hamilton. This gives us three possible sources for the design: the print, the gem, and the original vase. However, the important point is that the subject matter was available to Wedgwood in several forms and that he made use of it. The three figures from the vase appear together in pottery, singly and in pairs.

Three Dancing Graces. Illustrated in Rathbone, *Old Wedgwood,* Pl. LVI. These fully clothed dancing female figures were derived from a wall painting [99] from the Maison Dorée. It is probable that Wedgwood saw at least one edition of the publication of Bartoli, Bellori, and La Chausse, *Picturae Antiquae et Sepulcri Nasonum,* Rome, 1750, from which he also seems to have adapted many other designs as *Night Scattering Poppies, Nymphs Watering Pegasus, Aerial Figure,* etc. These dancing figures appear in Plate V of the first section of the publication.

HERCULANEUM FIGURES

These are listed in the French *Catalogue* of 1788 as follows:

Figures modelled after the paintings found in the ruins of Herculaneum and of which the models have been brought here by the Marquis of Lansdowne.

51
52
53
54   } Dancing Nymphs
55
56

57
58   } Centaurs
59

60 — Polyphemus
61 — Marsyas and the young Olympe
62 — Papyrius and his mother
64 — Bacchic figure
65 — ditto

Meteyard says of these subjects in *Life*, II, p. 371, "Besides these . . . were others called Herculaneum pictures. These were generally elongated slabs in the black basalts body or coloured black on the biscuit on which were painted in encaustic colours mythological scenes, Bacchanalian scenes, or aerial figures. The smaller articles of this character were intended as pictures for dressing-rooms or for ornamenting writing tables, cabinets . . . Unwin, Catherine Wilcox, Dovoto, and, at a later day . . . Aaron Steel, were employed in painting these Herculaneum pictures . . . There were also what were called ivory Herculaneum pictures, that is, the white biscuit reliefs and ground were covered over with a peculiar glaze . . . which upon firing imparted all the appearance of the finest ivory."

Of the *Dancing Nymphs*, which shall be treated first, Meteyard illustrates three in *Memorials of Wedgwood*, Pl. VII. One of the *Dancers* [100] is discussed separately from the other two. "Oval

Plate 45. Herculaneum figure. *Source.*

medallion. Basalts. 10 x 7 inches. They [Herculaneum figures] were made at Etruria prior to 1733 as they occur in the first and subsequent editions of the *Catalogue,* and not only in basalts, in white terra-cotta, and biscuit but at a later date in pale blue and white jasper. In this latter body they are very charming. They appear to have been impressed from clay moulds and then under-

Plate 46. Herculaneum figures. *Source.*

cut." This is a bewreathed female dancer playing cymbals over her left shoulder. Plate 45 is the original from Pompeii, which was found in the House of Cicero.[101] There is such a plaque in the Fogg Museum, no. 28 in the *Winthrop Bequest Catalogue of Old Wedgwood.*

The other two Herculaneum figures, plates 46, 47 and 48, in Meteyard's Pl. VII, see above, are also oval medallions, thirteen inches high. The field is black; the relief is white biscuit. Meteyard says of them, "These figures were made in various bodies and sizes. In the Catalogue they are described as Bacchanalian; but there is nothing Bacchic about them. The one is intended for Hebe, the

Plate 47. Herculaneum figure. *Wedgwood plaque.*

Plate 48. Herculaneum figure. *Wedgwood plaque.*

other for Nemesis or Pomona." The latter, called "Nemesis or Pomona" by Meteyard, in the original mural carries a branch with fruit on it in her right hand, an alabastron-shaped bottle in the left; she dances left with her drapery billowing behind. She, too, is from Pompeii, from the House of Cicero.[102] Meteyard, *Life*, II, p. 339 ff., says of this "danzatrice," "It . . . represents Pomona, the goddess of gardens and fruits. The figure which is aerial, descends towards the earth, bearing in one hand a cluster of fruit, in the other a short wand. The drapery is exquisitely rendered; the relief strongly undercut and the whole emblematic of motion and grace. The figure is said to have been modelled by Flaxman, and certainly bears the impress of his hand. Yet, if it is intended to represent *Pomona,* it is not named as such in any of the *Catalogues.*" The short wand described above is the alabastron which is completely omitted in another version, illustrated in Meteyard, *Memorials of Wedgwood,* Pl. VII. The identification of the figure as Pomona is probably due to the branch, but the alternate identification as Nemesis, who usually is accompanied by a bridle and wheel, is a little farfetched.

The so-called "Hebe," is probably so identified by Meteyard because she carries a pitcher. In the original [103] she also bears a plate with pieces of fruit on it. This is sometimes omitted in the Wedgwood, but an example of her bearing both, executed in black basalt, can be seen in Grant, *Makers of Black Basaltes,* Pl. XLIX, no. 1. The wall painting from which this is copied was found in Pompeii, also in the House of Cicero.[104] It is interesting to note that this figure is used in the ceiling of the "Japanned Room" in the Queen's House designed by the brothers Adam [105] in 1773.

As for the Bacchanalian character of these three figures which is denied by Meteyard, it is upheld by many scholars, one [106] of whom called the originals thereof "Menadi Danzati." They naturally do not appear in the *Catalogue* under the names given by Meteyard but under the general class of figures from Herculaneum as seen above.

Another of the Wedgwood Herculaneum figures illustrated in Grant, *Makers of Black Basaltes,* Pl. LI, is also a "danzatrice." Half-naked, she holds her billowing garment over her head with her right hand and carries a tray close to her hip with her left. The original, Plate 49,[107] is also from the House of Cicero in Pompeii.[108]

Plate 49. Herculaneum figure. *Source.*

Of the centaurs listed under this class, two can be definitely identified. One is the centaur with the young Dionysus and is discussed under the heading of *Dionysus.* The other can be seen in pottery in Barnard, *Chats on Wedgwood Ware,* p. 121, no. 3, and in Grant, *Makers of Black Basaltes,* Pl. XLIX, no. 4. The composition consists of a female centaur carrying a woman on her back who holds a thyrsus. The passenger faces away from the observer. The original is also a wall painting [109] found in the House of Cicero in Pompeii.[110]

No. 60 of Class II of the French *Catalogue* of 1788 is *Polyphemus* awaiting a message from his beloved, Galatea, which is carried to him by an eros. He sits, half-nude, holds a lyre in his left hand and stretches out his right to receive the messenger. The original painting [111] from Herculaneum [112] and now in the Naples Museum is reproduced in biscuit and can be seen in Barnard, *Chats on Wedgwood Ware*, p. 121.

The two Bacchic figures, nos. 64 and 65 in Class II of the French *Catalogue* of 1788, can be seen in pottery in Barnard, *Chats on Wedgwood Ware*, p. 121, in black basalt and are now in the Victoria and Albert Museum. The originals are two Dionysiac figures [113] from Herculaneum. In the original both are in gray monochrome. One wears a chlamys and carries a leaf and torch; [114] the other carries a thyrsus and taenia. As the ancient figures were enclosed in round frames, they were admirably suited to adaptation for Wedgwood's circular plaques.

So, as can be seen in the study of sources, many of the so-called Herculaneum figures are not from Herculaneum but from Pompeii. They are reproduced, in general, quite faithfully and are in many of the wares. They were already popular motifs used often in interior decoration [115] and therefore familiar to the buying public. They must have sold very well indeed, as at least one of them is listed in the first edition of the *Catalogue* and all in the last edition.

Plate 50. Death of Meleager, called "Death of a Roman Warrior."
Wedgwood plaque.

DEATH OF MELEAGER CALLED
"DEATH OF A ROMAN WARRIOR"
Plates 50 and 51

Illustrated in Meteyard, *Wedgwood and His Works,* Pl. VI, no. 2.
This subject, Plate 50, one of the eighty-two bas-reliefs of the first
Wedgwood Catalogue, is also no. 72, Class II, of the French *Catalogue* of 1788, in which it is described as after an ancient sarcophagus in Rome. Miss Meteyard, *Life,* II, p. 359, in her discussion of Plate VI, no. 2, shows a degree of confusion regarding the
source. She states, "The original bas-relief, of which this is a copy,
was one of several adorning a sarcophagus discovered near Rome
in the early part of the eighteenth century. In this was found the
celebrated vase known as the Barberini; an inscription testified
that the sarcophagus had contained the ashes of the Emperor Alexander Severus and his mother Julia Mamaea. . . . This tablet
appears in the first edition of the Catalogue, and Wedgwood was
probably indebted to Lord Cathcart or Sir William Hamilton for
a print or cast of the original bas-relief." This subject does not

Plate 51. Death of Meleager. *Source.*

appear on the so-called Sarcophagus of Alexander Severus which had on it scenes from the life of Achilles. The so-called Sarcophagus of Alexander Severus was first mentioned in the sixteenth century and bears no inscription identifying it; nor was the Barberini Vase found in the sarcophagus.[116]

This particular relief is a scene from the story of Meleager when the dead body of the hero is carried home by his friends. The original Greek marble relief,[117] Plate 51, is in the Stanza dei Filosofi in the Capitoline Museum and dates from the second half of the second century. The shoulders of Meleager are supported by an armed warrior and his feet by a man in a short tunic. A boy supports on his shoulders the thighs of the dead man. An elderly man is standing behind the body and holds Meleager's left hand. Underneath the group is a shield. In the background to the right is the figure of a woman. The original relief is smeared with plaster so that it is impossible to say whether it was originally continued at either end. It probably was, for in other representations of this group on sarcophagi it forms but part of the whole design.[118] Another use of it by a contemporary of Wedgwood can be seen at David Garrick's Villa in Hampton, Middlesex, where it was used by Robert Adam [119] as a decorative medallion on the landing as early as 1774.

The Wedgwood tablet presents a number of difficulties in the matter of source. The bas-relief in the Capitoline Museum forms only part of the pottery tablet, and changes have been made in it. The general attitudes of the main figures remain exactly the same, but much has been added. The faces of the supporting warrior and the supine hero are effaced in the original and therefore those had to be restored. A helmet is put on the head of the elderly man holding Meleager's hand. Two other helmeted men are put into the background of the main group, but the female is omitted. To the left of the central group are three men, one a youth whose back is to the observer. This youth can be seen in Plate 12 of Bartoli and Bellori's *Admiranda Romanarum Antiquarum . . .* published in 1693. It is probable that Wedgwood possessed this volume as he possessed other works of Bartoli and Bellori and that he derived this figure from the plate. There can be no doubt that this figure in Wedgwood's "Death of a Roman Warrior" is the same as the youth from the monument of Hadrian published in the seventeenth-century work. Another interesting figure in this pottery relief is the one on the extreme right, of a bearded man in a draped toga, resting his hand on a shield. This figure seems to derive its body from one of the men in the *Procession of Senators* [120] from the north side of the Ara Pacis of Augustus. This slab is now in the Uffizi. These slabs are badly mutilated, and the heads are restored. The man in pottery and the man in stone wear togas of identical drape, that is, covering the shoulder and draped across the diaphragm, showing the under garment. In his left hand, the Senator of the Ara Pacis seems to hold a scroll; in pottery he rests his right hand on a shield. The head supplied by the potter is that of a middle-aged bearded type. This figure occurs again in the Wedgwood plaque called "A Roman Procession."

This early basalt bas-relief affords a perfect example of the use of a classical art vocabulary. A central group from part of a sarcophagus, one figure from a Hadrianic relief and another from the Augustan Ara Pacis—all are used. Some of the elements recur in other representations.

MUCIUS SCAEVOLA

Illustrated in Meteyard, *Memorials of Wedgwood,* Pl. III, called "Captive Soldiers"; Rathbone, *Old Wedgwood,* Pl. LI; and Meteyard, *Choice Examples of Wedgwood Art,* Pl. XVI. It represents Mucius Scaevola flanked by two soldiers before King Porsena. Mucius Scaevola is putting his hand into the fire. This has been taken from a gem, probably from a Tassie impression [121] although it also appears in three books [122] known to serve as sources for the Wedgwood ware. Meteyard states definitely in her discussion of Plate XVI, that the subjects in the frame of cameos illustrated are chiefly from Tassie's pastes. An impression can be seen in the Boggs Collection in the Walters Art Gallery, Baltimore, drawer FF, no. 1794.

MUSES

In most ancient works only three Muses are found, and their attributes are musical instruments such as the flute, lyre, or barbiton. They are the daughters of Zeus and Mnemosyne. Later there are nine associated with Apollo, who in his capacity as leader of the choir of nine Muses is called *Musagetes*. The Muses are:

1. *Calliope,* chief of the Muses, Muse of epic poetry; she is represented with a tablet and stylus or sometimes with a roll of papers.

2. *Clio,* the Muse of history; she is represented sometimes sitting, with an open roll of paper or an open chest of books.

3. *Euterpe,* Muse of lyric poetry; she is represented with a flute or double flute.

4. *Melpomene,* Muse of tragedy; she is represented by a tragic mask, the club of Heracles or a sword; her head is surrounded with vine leaves, and she wears the cothurnus.

5. *Terpsichore,* the Muse of choral dance and song; she is represented with the lyre and plectrum.

6. *Erato,* the Muse of erotic poetry and mimic imitation; she is also represented with the lyre.

7. *Polymnia* or *Polyhymnia,* the Muse of the sublime hymn; she is represented in a pensive or meditating attitude.

8. *Urania,* the Muse of astronomy; she is represented with a globe and a little staff for indicating the course of the stars.

9. *Thalia,* the Muse of comedy and idyllic poetry; she is represented with a comic mask, a shepherd's staff and a wreath of ivy.

The Muses were sometimes represented with plumes on their heads as trophies of their victory over the sirens but this characteristic is not found in Wedgwood's Muse types.

A bill of January 3, 1775, signed by John Flaxman, Jr., for his father, mentions the figures of Melpomene, Thalia, Terpsichore, and Euterpe. The elder Flaxman was a dealer in plaster casts, and these were probably casts of ancient statues.

In 1776, Flaxman was commissioned to model six of the nine

Muses. But the order was countermanded. Wedgwood writes to Bentley, Oct. 29, 1777, "Having laid all our bas-relief Goddesses upon their backs upon a board, in order to increase their number, I instantly perceived the six Muses we want might be produced from this lovely group at half the trouble and expense they could be procured from Flaxman and much better figures. For little more than 5s. we can complete them very well. I hope you have

Plate 52. Sarcophagus of the Muses. *Source.*

not order'd them to be model'd as I desired you would; but if you have, so be it, it is only so much loss . . ." The countermand was too late, and Flaxman completed this group. This explains the fact that there are different versions of the same Muse and also why it is so hard to differentiate between the Muses. There are the casts obtained from the elder Flaxman in 1775; there are the Goddesses mentioned in the letter of 1776; and there is the group of Flaxman's Muses. It is also quite likely that the statues of the Goddesses used were not all those of Muses but that the attributes were added later.

In the last edition of the *Catalogue,* the French edition of 1788, the nine Muses and Apollo are numbers 214–223 in Class II, Bas-reliefs, Medallions and Tablets. It is not mentioned that they are by John Flaxman nor is any other source given.

In treating the Muses, only those types which have been found to have definite ancient roots are discussed. Some of these are attributed to Flaxman as shall be seen.

Polymnia or *Polyhymnia.* The type of this Muse is that derived from the Polymnia of the Sarcophagus of the Muses,[123] Plate 52, now in the Salle des Caryatides of the Louvre which was formerly in the Albani Collection, then in the Capitoline Museum. The sarcophagus is in almost perfect condition; it is of Pentelic marble and belonged to the family of Atius. This funerary monument was evidently a famous one as it appears in the library at Mellerstain[124] by Adam (1770–1778), Berwickshire. Polymnia faces left on the sarcophagus, though in Wedgwood she faces either way. She leans on a rocky column, chin resting on right hand, left wrapped in her garment.

There is also a series of gems modelled after the Muse of the sarcophagus, one of which is signed by Pichler,[125] perhaps no. 3490 of Raspe, p. 336.

In Wedgwood ware, Plate 53, the use of Polymnia can be illustrated by a jasper pitcher, no. 23.301, a basalt vase, no. 95.265, and a jasper vase, no. 25.282, in the Museum of Fine Arts, Boston, and by Plate XLV in Rathbone, *Old Wedgwood*.

This Muse, now called "Hope," is also seen leaning on an anchor on gems [126] and has been used for small pottery cameos seen in jewelry such as that illustrated in Barnard, *Chats on Wedgwood Ware*, p. 188, where it is part of a bracelet now in the Etruria Museum; and for separate medallions such as that black and white jasper one illustrated in Rathbone, *Old Wedgwood*, Pl. LVIII. This series was probably derived from Tassie as he lists and illustrates [127] this type. Tassie is supposed to have directed the making of this type so that Wedgwood no doubt used a Tassie impression to obtain his pottery cameo.

Melpomene. There are two types of Melpomene derived from the antique used by Wedgwood. The first is the Muse from the Sarcophagus of the Muses, Plate 52, in the Louvre. Her tragic mask is pushed up on her head and worn as a hat. She carries no club. One foot rests upon a rocky elevation; her right elbow rests upon her right knee. There is a gem signed by Heckert [128] modelled after the Melpomene of the sarcophagus. In pottery she can be seen on a lilac jasper plaque in the collection of the author.

The second type, Plate 53, is from a painting [129] of a statue from Pompeii now in the Louvre.[130] She wears a blue chiton, stands on a console on which is written in Greek, "Melpomene, Tragedian."

Plate 53. Muses. *Wedgwood vase.*

She carries the club of Heracles in one hand and the tragic mask in the other. This type can be seen in Wedgwood ware in Pl. XXIII, group 2, and Pl. XXVI, group 2, in Meteyard, *Wedgwood and His Works;* on a jasper pitcher, no. 23.301, and basalt vase, no. 95.265, in the Museum of Fine Arts, Boston; and in Plates XII and XLV in Rathbone, *Old Wedgwood.* In the house of Lord Wemyss, no. 64 Queen Street, Edinburgh, this figure appears in plaster in a frieze under the ceiling of one of the rooms.[131] This house, if not by the Adams themselves, is "Adamistic" in style and dates from about 1791.

Thalia. There is only one type of Thalia used, and she is derived from a wall painting from Pompeii now in the Louvre.[132] She wears a wreath and green chiton. She stands on a console on which is written in Greek, "Thalia, Comedian." In her right hand she carries the shepherd's staff and in her left the comic mask. In jasper ware she may be seen on a pitcher, green jasper, white relief, in the author's collection; in Pl. XXVI, group 2, in Meteyard, *Wedgwood and His Works;* on a vase in the Museum of Fine Arts, Boston; no. 95.260, and in Pl. XII in Rathbone, *Old Wedgwood.*

Euterpe. The type of Euterpe used by Wedgwood derives ultimately from the antique. She faces right, leans on a column; her left hand under her chin holds a double pipe. The source is a gem [133] signed by Pichler. It is root of emerald and was in the collection of a Mr. Morrison. Pichler was inspired by ancient works of art and made copies of them on engraved gems.[134] In this case he was inspired by the reverse of a coin issued by Quintus Pomponius Musa,[135] about 72 B.C. It is one of a series intended to refer to the cognomen of the moneyer. Wedgwood probably bought the Tassie impression of this gem. This series of coins is illustrated right beneath the Sarcophagus of the Muses in Montfaucon's *Antiquité Expliquée,* I, 1, Pl. LIX. Euterpe is illustration number 11 on that plate. It is known that the Montfaucon publication was known to Wedgwood, so that this illustration may have inspired him directly. However, as it is rather small and not very detailed, it is logical to assume that the Pichler gem offered the model of this lovely Muse type in pottery.

In pottery this Muse may be seen on a black and white jasper vase, no. B 140, in the British Museum, on a vase in the Museum of Fine Arts, Boston, no. 95.260, and in blue and white jasper in Pl. IX in Meteyard, *Memorials of Wedgwood*. This medallion is attributed to Flaxman. Miss Meteyard states about this and companion medallions of Muses, "These figures differ from their antique representatives—Euterpe, the muse of lyric poetry, being a seated figure with a single pipe or flute resting in her left hand. . . ." Among the ancient representations of Euterpe, there are both standing and sitting versions as there is no fixed rule. She very often carries a double pipe or two pipes as she is generally accredited with the invention of the double flute. Miss Meteyard's comments in this case can be discounted especially in view of the original source of this design.

Urania. The type of Urania used by Wedgwood is adapted directly from the Muse on the Sarcophagus of the Muses in the Louvre (Plate 52). Urania leans her head on her left arm, which in turn rests upon a column. Her right hand holds a staff with which she points to the globe at her feet. There is also an eighteenth-century engraved chalcedony [136] signed in Greek letters "Pichler," inspired by this Muse.

In pottery, she may be seen on a green and white jasper pitcher in the collection of the author; on a black and white jasper vase, no. B 140, in the British Museum; on a bulb-grower vase in the British Museum; on a vase and a pitcher, no. 95.260 and 23.301, in the Museum of Fine Arts, Boston; illustrated in Pl. XII in Rathbone, *Old Wedgwood*.

Terpsichore. There are two versions of Terpsichore. The first is taken from the Sarcophagus of the Muses in the Louvre. She faces right, carries a lyre, wears a flowing robe and has a wreath on her head. In jasper she can be seen on a lilac and white plaque in the collection of the author.

The second type labelled "Terpsichore" by Wedgwood is that of a maiden carrying a lyre, facing right and leaning against a column on which is a statue. The original is an antique yellow paste,[137] once belonging to the Abbé Pietro Andreini and then to the Medici family, signed in Greek letters as by Onesas. It is called *Erato* by Baron de Stosch.[138] There are many versions of this maiden and lyre, most of them eighteenth-century. There is one signed by L. Pichler.[139] There are many versions [140] listed in the Raspe *Catalogue* including the Pichler version, the Medici gem; others belonged to the Strozzi family,[141] to de Stosch himself, and to a Baron de Gleichen.[142] Only the Medici gem is considered antique.[143] There are several of the later versions in the British Museum.[144] In Wedgwood, there is an example illustrated in Meteyard, *Memorials of Wedgwood*, Pl. IV.

Erato. This Muse, because she too is represented with a lyre, has been interchanged with Terpsichore, as in the case of the maiden with the lyre illustrated in Meteyard, *Memorials of Wedgwood*, Pl. IX, who is identified as Terpsichore and discussed under that Muse. The one version of the gem has been called Erato by Baron de Stosch.

There is the dancer from the Dionysiac frieze of the Borghese Vase who appears on a Wedgwood vase as a Muse, as illustrated in Meteyard, *Wedgwood and His Works*, Pl. XII, group 2. She might be a representation of Erato, who although usually identified as the Muse of erotic poetry is also associated with Dionysiac music. She offers another example of the lack of understanding of ancient monuments and their iconography.

Calliope. Though Calliope is the Muse of epic poetry and is usually represented with a tablet and stylus, one version used is inspired by one of the coins of Quintus Pomponius Musa [145] on which she carries a lyre also. She wears a long flowing garment which billows out behind her. She faces right and plays her lyre which rests upon a column or pedestal. She can be seen in pottery in Pl. XXVI, group 2, in Meteyard, *Wedgwood and His Works;* illustrated in Pls. XXIX and XLV of Rathbone, *Old Wedgwood;* on a basalt vase, no. 95.265, in the Museum of Fine Arts, Boston.

Another type, and an interesting one, is found on a vase illustrated in Meteyard, *Wedgwood and His Works*, Pl. XXVI, group 2, and on a jasper pitcher, no. 23.302, in the Museum of Fine Arts, Boston. It is a dancing figure holding the attributes of Calliope, stylus and paper. It has evidently been inspired by the "Borghese Dancers," [146] probably the second figure from the right.

Clio. There are several types of Clio, but only one has been found to have an exact ancient derivation. She also comes from the Sarcophagus of the Muses in the Louvre. Clio holds a paper in her left hand and leans on a column. Her right arm is crossed over her breast and is covered except for the hand. This can be seen on a vase illustrated in Meteyard, *Wedgwood and His Works*, Pl. XXII, group 2.

Plate 54. Nereids. *Source.*

NEREIDS
Plate 54

Illustrated in Meteyard, *Memorials of Wedgwood,* Pl. XXIV; a plaque 21⁷⁄₁₆ by 6 inches. ". . . said to have been modelled by Henry Webber when . . . he was in Rome, sometime within the period 1779–1781." It is one of the unrecorded bas-reliefs. Miss Meteyard also thinks that it is in the style of Pacetti. Its source is a Pentelic marble sarcophagus, Plate 54,[147] once in the collection of the Capitoline Museum and now in the Louvre. The relief of the pottery is rather low and there is a somewhat dry look to the composition which in the original was an exciting procession of sea people. The design has been copied faithfully and consists of sea nymphs and tritons riding strange combinations of animals such as a goat that has a fish tail, accompanied by *erotes* who ride dolphins and generally sport about.

NIGHT SHEDDING POPPIES

Illustrated in Meteyard, *Memorials of Wedgwood,* Pl. XIV. And also vase no. 95.259 in the Museum of Fine Arts, Boston. A sea-green jasper vase with white relief, 11 inches high. "Beautifully ornamented with signs of the zodiac, floral wreaths and medallions, of which the subjects, taken from gems, are two variations of 'Night Shedding Poppies.' " The first consists of a lovely floating figure holding in one hand a container of blossoms, in the other a wreath. Over her shoulder another graceful figure reaches out as if to take a blossom and with the other hand holds a wreath over her own head.[148] Swirling drapery and clouds add to the already delightfully aerial effect. The other variation is a winged single figure [149] holding a wreath over her head. The originals of these two designs are not gems but wall paintings from the Esquiline in Rome and have been reproduced faithfully in the pottery.

NYMPHS DECORATING THE
STATUE OF PRIAPUS
Plate 55

Illustrated in Meteyard, *Memorials of Wedgwood,* Pl. X. Oval medallion; jasper, pale blue ground, white relief; 87/8 inches by 7 inches. "This subject was modelled by Webber sometime between 1782 and 1794. The head of Priapus is taken from an antique gem or bas-relief. . . . The female figures are essentially modern." A fact evidently unknown to Miss Meteyard is that this design was originally executed by Angelica Kauffman, engraved by Bartolozzi, and was a most popular subject in classicizing England. A Derby biscuit group [150] modelled by Spengler, dated 1795, and a Worcester dessert dish [151] painted by Humphrey Chamberlin, dated 1800, both in the Victoria and Albert Museum, also use the identical subject matter. It is interesting to note that there is also an eighteenth-century gem [152] having this design, but in it the two nymphs are nude. It is signed by G. Pichler. In this case, as in so many others, the design utilized by Wedgwood is by no means original but is a well-known composition on whose popularity the potter could capitalize when he translated it into jasper.

Plate 55. Nymphs decorating the statue of Priapus. *Wedgwood plaque.*

Plate 56. Orestes and Pylades. *Wedgwood plaque.*

ORESTES AND PYLADES
Plate 56

Illustrated in Meteyard, *Wedgwood and His Works*, Pl. II. Bas-relief or oblong tablet; pale blue jasper, white relief; 22¼ inches by 7¾ inches. "Modelled by John Devaere for Wedgwood in Flaxman's atelier at Rome, between 1790 and 1793." The original [153] is a sarcophagus, once in the Palazzo Accoramboni and now in Munich.[154] The design of the Wedgwood plaque is a combination of the right-hand group of the front side, consisting of Iphigenia standing in front of a shrine, Orestes and Pylades bound and guarded by a barbarian, and one of the short sides showing Iphigenia giving them a letter while a barbarian holds up a shield. Of the many sarcophagi having these scenes and figures in almost identical attitudes, this one can be identified as the definite source because of the minutely correct re-representation, in pottery, of the grove of the goddess. It is a small covered shrine upheld by two pillars; a tree in the back of it branches out across its side; a bovine skull and a scabbard are bound to the tree. The goddess stands on a pedestal within the shrine while from the corners of it hang two human heads. The original is slightly defaced, especially the two figures of Orestes and Pylades from the short side. Devaere has used the figures that are complete from the other side, merely reversing them. This can be seen in the use of the nude male figure with one hand on his chin. The nude bodies of the males have been skillfully draped so that they will not offend. Artistically, it appears to be one of the more successful examples of the repetition of ancient works.

Plate 57. The Judgment of Paris. *Wedgwood plaque.*

PARIS

The Judgment of Paris, Plate 57. Illustrated in Meteyard, *Wedgwood and His Works,* Pl. III, no. 3. Bas-relief or tablet; black jasper, white relief; 7 by 18½ inches. "This tablet in a small form . . . appears in the first and second editions of the catalogue. It was remodelled on a larger scale for Wedgwood by Flaxman between 1775 and 1777 and is numbered 183 in the fourth edition of the *Catalogue* published in the latter year. Another version seems to have been modelled in 1790–1791 by Devaere whilst at work in Flaxman's atelier in Rome." Considering the size of this plaque and the amount of technical proficiency required to fire such a large pottery relief, it is here suggested that this is the later version by Devaere, which was made when all the problems of shrinkage, etc., would have been settled successfully. The source for this very ambitious pottery plaque is the long side of a black-veined marble sarcophagus [155] from the Villa Pamphili in Rome. There are eight figures taken from this and used in the jasper ware. Three partially draped source-nymphs appear on the left. Paris, wearing his Phrygian cap and accompanied by his dog, is seated under a tree. Hermes, wearing his winged hat and bearing the caduceus, offers him the apple. Next appear the three goddesses: Aphrodite accompanied by a small eros, nude except for a billowing drapery; Hera, wearing a diadem, completely clothed with part of her mantle over her head; Athena, carrying a spear, wearing a helmet and with her shield resting behind her. Various background figures, sheep and cows have been omitted in the Wedgwood version. The original sarcophagus is in rather bad condition so that many details of clothing, position, and physiognomy have been left to the discretion of the artist. It is one of the most satisfactory of all the Wedgwood plaques, having two side groups and a central point of interest with none of the cluttered quality of the original relief. The white figures are silhouetted beautifully against the black background, forming a pleasant contrast. This is an excellent example of the good adaptation of a classic model into pottery.

Paris and Helen Ill-advised, on a black and white jasper vase in the Walters Art Gallery, Baltimore. Helen is seated next to Aphrodite, who has her arm about Helen. To the right is a standing group consisting of a winged eros with one arm about the shoulder of Paris, who wears a cloak and points upward with the left hand. At the extreme left of the composition is a large pedestal with a crowned, veiled female figure seated on the edge, her right hand resting upon the back of a dove. She is identified as the goddess of Persuasion [156] in the description of the original Greek marble relief [157] found in Rome and now in the museum in Naples. Over each figure in the original are identifying names in Greek. This design is used by the Wedgwood factory today and appears not only in jasper ware but also in the modern cream ware, in which the figures often are in blue and pink.

Plate 58. Pegasus cared for by Nymphs. *Wedgwood medallion.*

PEGASUS

Pegasus and Bellerophon. Illustrated in Rathbone, *Catalogue of the Wedgwood Museum,* p. 102. Pegasus appears with Bellerophon, who waters him at the fountain Hippocrene, on one [158] of the eight reliefs found at S. Agnese and now in the Palazzo Spada. Wace [159] believes that the artist has borrowed an older motif and given his own rendering, pointing out the similar groups found on a sarcophagus at Athens and an ivory box from Veroli. The original source was perhaps a painting. The landscape is handled well, the rocky elevation and the three balancing each other. However, Pegasus is on too small a scale. Bellerophon is seen in profile and recalls the Polycleitan Doryphorus. Wace dates this relief about 130 A.D.

There is a gem illustrated in Lippold, *Gemmen,* Pl. CXLIV, no. 3; another is in the Walters Art Gallery, Baltimore. Tassie made an impression of a gem of this design, an example of which is in the Boggs Collection of Tassie Impressions, drawer CC, no.

1611, which is no. 9052 in the Raspe *Catalogue*. It is reproduced faithfully in the Wedgwood ware.

Pegasus cared for by Nymphs, Plate 58. Illustrated in Rathbone, *Old Wedgwood,* Pl. XLVII. Pegasus and three nymphs stand in a stream. One nymph holds a jar; another, kneeling, holds a forefoot of the winged horse while the third strokes his chin. The original is a wall painting [160] from the Tomb of the Nasonii. It is most probable that Wedgwood derived the design from one of his source books in which it appeared, e.g., Bartoli, Bellori and La Chausse, *Picturae Antiquae et Sepulcri Nasonum,* Pl. XX of the second part. All three nymphs have acquired drapery, whereas in the mural all were naked above the waist. This painting forms part of the decoration of the west back wall of the tomb of the Nasonii near the station *ad Rubras* about five miles north of Rome on the Via Flaminia. The Tomb was discovered in 1674 and its decoration copied by Pietro Santi Bartoli and published with an explanatory text by Bellori.[161] The paintings were already faded and spoiled by damp as early as 1680. Bartoli has added landscape backgrounds and other details which do not occur in the originals.[162] Since the paintings were in bad condition by the time of Wedgwood, it is logical to assume that he worked from the prints. Indeed, the details of the figures and their drapery, the landscape background, all point to the engraving rather than to the painting. Except for the clothing of the nymphs mentioned above, the entire composition has been reproduced faithfully.

PERSEUS AND ANDROMEDA
Plate 59

Illustrated in Meteyard, *Life of Josiah Wedgwood*, II, p. 461.
There is a famous bas-relief [163] of this subject found with two
others in the Piazza SS. Apostoli in digging the foundations of the
Palazzo Muti. It was afterwards in the Villa Pamfili, Albani Collection, and now is in the Stanza degli Imperatori of the Capitoline
Museum. It was reproduced on gems [164] in the eighteenth century,
and an impression of such a gem can be seen in the Boggs Collection of Tassie Impressions in the Walters Art Gallery, Baltimore,
drawer FFF, no. 3381.[165] This subject was probably supplied Wedgwood by Tassie as it appears in gem size in pottery.

Andromeda steps down from the rock. Her left hand is supported by Perseus' right hand. Perseus stands to the left in a statu-
esque attitude, his left hand behind him. His chlamys rests on his
left shoulder and is wrapped around the left arm. The sea mon-
ster is under the foot of Andromeda. The date of the original
relief is undecided, some authorities believing it Alexandrian,
others Augustan. But the Roman workmanship seems to date it
about the second century A.D.[166] This composition, *Perseus and
Andromeda,* was used previously in a medallion in the Entrance
Hall of Syon House by Robert Adam about 1763.[167]

Plate 59. Perseus and Andromeda. *Source.*

Plate 60. Procession of the Deities. *Wedgwood vase.*

Plate 61. Procession of the Deities. *Source.*

PROCESSION OF DEITIES
Plates 60 and 61

Illustrated in Meteyard, *Memorials of Wedgwood,* Pl. XIV. "The vases . . . are of red terra-cotta; the ornaments black; height, 15 inches. Their form is excellent. The bas-relief figures appear to be processional, and are clearly Egyptian rather than Greek." The source of this design is the *Puteal of the Twelve Gods* [168] now in the Galleria of the Capitoline Museum. The reliefs have given rise to many interpretations, but in each case the precedence and position given to the gods remain inexplicable. It is accepted that the work is late, probably Athenian, first century B.C., but repeats early fifth-century types. It was formerly in the collection of the Medici and then in that of Cardinal Albani. Its provenance is uncertain. Miss Meteyard was perhaps not familiar with all aspects of Greek art when she assigned the relief to the Egyptians.

Plate 62. Procession to Isis. *Wedgwood plaque.*

PROCESSION TO ISIS
Plate 62

Illustrated in Meteyard, *Memorials of Wedgwood,* Pl. XX. Plaque
in ordinary earthenware thickly coated with black glaze. "It is undoubtedly one of Wedgwood's early trial pieces in encaustic
painting. The subject taken from an Egyptian vase, is considered
by a great classical authority to be most archaic and interesting."
The original of this plaque is not an Egyptian vase but a Hadrianic relief [169] once in the Mattei Collection, now in the Cortile de
Belvedere of the Vatican. It has four figures, facing right, in high
relief, who are evidently part of a procession to Isis. They carry a
sistrum, vase, scroll, and snake respectively. This is undoubtedly
an archaic Wedgwood plaque but not an archaic ancient work,
having been assigned to the Hadrianic period, one of a great
renaissance in art.

Plate 63. Roman Procession. *Wedgwood plaque.*

ROMAN PROCESSION
Plate 63

Illustrated in Meteyard, *Memorials of Wedgwood,* Pl. XXI. Bas-relief tablet in basalt. 20 by 9¼ inches. "This fine bas-relief is a continuation of the tablet well known as the 'Death of a Roman Warrior'. . . . The original bas-relief, containing in contiguity the two tablets, forms part of an ancient sarcophagus in Rome or Florence. The first tablet was manufactured by Wedgwood prior to 1773, the second . . . not until far later, it being modelled from the original between 1788 and 1795 by either Pacetti or Dalmazzoni. It forms one among the long list of unrecorded bas-reliefs."

This basalt relief may be a continuation of the Wedgwood *Death of a Roman Warrior* but it does not form any part of the original sarcophagus or of any sarcophagus. The source is the Ara Pacis of Augustus. It is not unrecorded, as a "Procession Romaine" is listed as no. 237 of Class II in the French *Catalogue* of 1788. The Ara Pacis Augustae [170] is a monument set up by the Senate in honor of the Emperor's victorious return from a double campaign, in Spain and Gaul. The altar occupied, in the Campus Martius, a space to the left, now to the west of the modern Corso, on the site of the modern Palazzo Ottaboni-Fiano. Fragments of the decoration sculptures have been found scattered in the Palazzo Fiano, the Vatican, Villa Medici, Uffizi, Louvre, and Vienna. On the walls were an allegorical group of Tellus, procession of the Emperor, attendants, and senators, and a sacrifice. Recently it has been re-erected on its original site.

It is convenient here to number the figures in the Wedgwood relief and to compare them with Plates XII and XIII of Strong, *Roman Sculpture.* They are numbered from left to right.

1. The first figure is the same one as the first figure of *The Death of a Roman Warrior* and therefore derives from the same source, i.e., Pl. 12 of Bartoli and Bellori, *Admiranda,* first figure from the left.

2. This figure derives from the Uffizi slab (Strong, *op. cit.,* Pl. XII) the third full figure from the left. He faces right and his right hand is wrapped in his toga. In the original he carries nothing in his other hand, but in the Wedgwood he bears a sprig of some variety. Wedgwood has also restored this head as bearded, and it is very reminiscent of the head of Figure No. 3.

3. This is the same as the man from the extreme right of *The Death of a Roman Warrior.* He is derived from the first figure of the Uffizi slab of the Ara Pacis, Strong, *op. cit.,* Pl. XIII. His head has been restored as bearded by Wedgwood's artist.

4. This figure has his mantle thrown over his head and his uncovered right arm crosses his chest to hold the part thrown over the head. The source is the fourth full figure from the left in the Uffizi slab, Strong, *op. cit.,* Pl. XII.

5 and 6. One Roman in the procession turns backward toward the man directly following him. These two figures derive from two figures on one of the Uffizi fragments, Strong, *op. cit.,* Pl. XIII.

7. This figure derives from the second figure from the left on one of the Uffizi slabs, Strong, *op. cit.,* Pl. XII. In the Wedgwood, his head is thrown backward a little.

8. The last figure in the Wedgwood procession derives from the

second figure from the right on one of the Uffizi slabs, Strong, *op. cit.*, Pl. XII.

It is important to note the differences between the Wedgwood version and the original which are minor but misleading. The heads that have been restored on the marble slabs differ from those used by the potter so that all the figures have been identified by position and the fall of the drapery. Details are added in the pottery that do not occur in the Roman relief, as the sprigs carried by the men. As most of the figures are copied from the Uffizi slabs, it seems logical that one of the artists in the atelier in Italy worked on the model for Wedgwood. It is one of the more jejune compositions in pottery, having none of the rhythmic breaks that the complete altar afforded.

Plate 64. Warrior and Nike. *Figures from a Wedgwood cup.*

SACRIFICES

It has often been said that Wedgwood produced so many different designs, all called merely "Sacrifice," that it is hard, even impossible, to determine the particular Wedgwood design designated, not to mention the source of it. This is completely true. Working, however, from figure arrangement rather than from the name of a composition, the author has been able to identify a few of the sources of the various designs under the general heading of "Sacrifice."

1. *Warrior and Nike,* Plate 64. Illustrated in Church, *Josiah Wedgwood, Master Potter,* p. 26, and Meteyard, *Wedgwood and His Works,* Pl. XIV. A helmeted warrior with his head bowed and left hand on his hip stands to one side of a statue of Athena around whose pedestal a serpent is twined. On the other side stands a winged victory bearing in one hand a palm leaf and in the other a plate from which the serpent drinks. The source of this is a bas-relief [171] now in the Louvre. The warrior has been variously identified as Themistocles, Cimon, or Philoctetes.[172] The relief is in the style of a choragic monument. In the original the warrior

holds a tuft of feathers, the symbol of a naval victory; this is changed to a spear in the pottery. The ancient bas-relief is badly effaced, but there is little doubt that it is the model for the eighteenth-century one. The shield behind the pedestal of the goddess, the position of the warrior, the drapery of the warrior, especially the piece that is blown out in front of him, are the same in both and bespeak model and source.

2. *Sacrifice.* Illustrated in Meteyard, *Life of Josiah Wedgwood,* II, p. 51. This composition of a seated man, two standing figures, and an altar, derives from a gem and was probably supplied by Tassie as an impression appears in the Boggs Collection of Tassie Impressions, Walters Art Gallery, Baltimore, drawer T, no. 1145. The original [173] was a gem in the Maffei Collection. It is admittedly modern, that is, sixteenth-century Italian Renaissance, but it is of fine workmanship. The original rock crystal is now in the British Museum and is thought to be by Valerio Belli.

3. *Sacrifice.* Illustrated in the *Sale Catalogue of Beautiful Old Wedgwood belonging to Horace Townsend,* no. 344, one of a frame of twenty-five cameos. It is of octagonal shape. A veiled figure holds a patera over an altar under a tree. This is no. 8371 in Raspe's *Catalogue,* and is an antique paste from the collection of the King of Prussia. An impression of this can be seen in the Boggs Collection of Tassie Impressions, Walters Art Gallery, Baltimore, drawer V, no. 1158.

4. *Sacrifice to Hymen.* Illustrated in the *Catalogue of the . . . Winthrop Bequest,* Fogg Museum, no. 19. A young woman empties her peplum over a lighted altar. This is no. 8362 in the Raspe *Catalogue,* which identifies it as in the style of Vicentino Belli, a Renaissance gem engraver. An impression exists in the Boggs Collection of Tassie Impressions, Walters Art Gallery, Baltimore, drawer V, no. 1163. Wedgwood added a shrine of Eros and a zodiac border to make, on the whole, a charming jasper cameo.

5. *Sacrifice.* Illustrated in Meteyard, *Memorials of Wedgwood,* Pl. XXIII, no. 3, and annotated: "This plaque seems to be Flaxman's interpretation of an 'Offering to Peace' modelled by him, probably from a gem, for 'Wedgwood and Bentley' between 1775

and 1777 and made at Etruria in several sizes." This is also what is called a "composition" piece, that is, each part or some parts derive from different sources and have been combined rather than the whole derived from one particular source. This is best explained by giving the sources of each figure, where they are known. The figures will be discussed from left to right. See Plate 34.

1 and 5. These figures probably derive from a figure in the Palladian Frieze in the Forum Transitorium as illustrated in Bartoli and Bellori, *Admiranda*, Pl. 40, the central figure. In no other figure is the drapery so similar, that is, an over-mantle ungirt. In both the print and in the Wedgwood the head is seen in profile, whereas in the original relief there are no head and arms as it is in bad condition. Figures 1 and 5 are fundamentally the same if one ignores the arms, which even in the print are not completely restored. In this case, it is the print, not the original bas-relief that supplied the motif.

2. The second figure in the Wedgwood *Sacrifice* derives from Bartoli and Bellori, *Admiranda*, Pl. 40, the end figure on the right. In this case, there can be little doubt, for the position of the hands is remarkably similar while the draping and knotting to one side of the garment are so exact as to preclude coincidence.

3. The Selene and Eros type are from the Sarcophagus of Gerontia in the Capitoline Museum.

6. This woman seated on a rocky elevation with a tree in front of her can be traced to the seated figure at the extreme right of Pl. 41 in Bartoli and Bellori, *Admiranda*.

7. This fully draped standing woman derives from the third figure from the left of Pl. 40 in Bartoli and Bellori, *Admiranda*.

8. The final figure in the Wedgwood *Sacrifice* relief leans upon a pedestal on which is a chubby Eros. A goat prances to the left at the foot of the pedestal. Although none of the figures in the Palladian Frieze as illustrated in Bartoli and Bellori, *Admiranda*, tally exactly, there seems to be a resemblance between this Wedgwood figure and the third figure from the left of Pl. 35. This figure also leans on a pedestal, left arm resting upon it.

It is important to emphasize that the source of these figures is not the actual frieze in the Forum Transitorium but drawings thereof, and the ancient figures appear in pottery through the medium of the prints. This can be seen when comparing the prints and the monument. The ancient relief has been badly mutilated, but in the print the figures' heads, arms, and drapery have been restored so freely that even the original sequence of figures has been ignored. The prints are really a hodgepodge deriving only vaguely from the original relief, and it is these prints which supplied the inspiration for many of the female-figure designs of Wedgwood. Another interesting and more complete use of the prints was made by the brothers Adam in the Round Room at Lansdowne House (1765–1766) where the entire restored frieze appears.[174] It was evidently a favorite composition of the Adams as it appears in the background of the frontispiece of their *Works* (1775).[175]

TALISMAN

Illustrated in Meteyard, *Memorials of Wedgwood,* Pl. III. A cameo set as a coat button. The subject is doubtful but Mariette, in his discussion of the original gem [176] in the collection of the King of France, says it is probably a Talisman. It too must have come to Wedgwood through a Tassie impression, and such an impression of this gem can be seen in the Boggs Collection of Tassie Impressions in the Walters Art Gallery, Baltimore, drawer E, no. 245. It consists of a seminude seated female figure holding a shield on which is a mask of Medusa. The shield rests upon a pedestal. There is a strange epigraphical combination of Roman and Greek letters on the pedestal and some Cuphic about the edge.

VOLUMNIA, MOTHER OF CORIOLANUS

Illustrated in Rathbone, *Old Wedgwood,* Pl. LXI. Mrs. Gorely in her thorough discussion of the sources of this design, points out that the original model for this is Vol. II, pl. 26, of d'Hancarville, a copy of which was given to Wedgwood by Sir Watkin Williams Wynn, and while Flaxman did model this design, it was after a print. There is in existence a second design which goes under the same name and has added to the confusion in identifying the sources and subject matter. Rathbone calls it *Penelope and Her Maidens.*

ZEUS AND HERA
(JUPITER AND JUNO)

Illustrated in Meteyard, *Wedgwood and His Works,* Pl. IX, nos.
2 and 3. Oval medallions; 7½ by 5 inches; blue and white jasper.
They are numbers 99 and 98 in Class II in the French *Catalogue*
of 1788. Meteyard, *Life,* II, p. 322, assigns them to Flaxman on
the basis of the bill of 1775 signed by Flaxman Jr. for his father.
Constable, *John Flaxman,* p. 15, states that it has been generally
accepted that this bill is for casts sold by the elder Flaxman to
Wedgwood. This makes it more probable that Wedgwood worked
directly from the casts of these two gods which are reliefs on the
base of a candelabrum [177] of fine-grained white marble in the
Galleria delle Statue of the Vatican. Found in the Villa of Hadrian, it became part of the Vatican Collection in 1770, and it is
an example of Hadrianic decorative art.[178] These two figures
naturally lend themselves very well to reproduction in jasper relief
as they were already in relief. They make a pair of very lovely
jasper medallions. Zeus stands nude except for his chlamys over
his left shoulder, facing right; in one hand he holds a thunderbolt
while the other leans upon a tall staff. Hera is completely draped,
wears a diadem, faces left, and also leans upon a staff.

Another representation of Hera or Juno is illustrated in
Meteyard, *Memorials of Wedgwood,* Pl. VIII, the medallion on
the lower left. Meteyard calls it "Tuccia, a vestal, carrying water
in a sieve in proof of her chastity." However, this design is derived from a gem,[179] an impression of which is in the Boggs Collection of Tassie Impressions, Walters Art Gallery, Baltimore, drawer
C, no. 168. It is not an antique gem but is definitely in the classic
mood. It is called "Juno and Her Peacock." The goddess, her
bosom bare, leans her back against a pedestal on which there is a
tripod. In her left hand she holds an egg-shaped object which
Meteyard assumes is the sieve. The bird is to the right of the god-

dess. The original gem is rather large, and the technique is rather sketchy. The Wedgwood version has been filled out; the figure of Hera has been rounded and is less elongated; the bird and drapery are better delineated.

[1] August Baumeister, *Denkmäler des Klassischen Altertums*, I, p. 4; J. D. Guigniaut, *Nouvelle Gallerie Mythologique Comprenant la Gallerie Mythologique de Feu A. L. Millin*, no. 764; H. S. Jones, *Catalogue of the Ancient Sculptures . . . of the Museo Capitolino*, Pl. 9; S. Reinach, *Répertoire de Reliefs Grecs et Romains*, III, p. 177; P. Righetti, *Descrizione del Campidoglio*, II, Pls. 277–280; W. H. Roscher, *Ausführliches Lexikon der Griechischen und Römischen Mythologie*, IV, 1575–1576.

[2] Jones, *op. cit.*, p. 47.

[3] *Ibid.*, p. 46.

[4] *Ibid.*, p. 45.

[5] Also illustrated in Meteyard, *Wedgwood and His Works*, Pl. XX, Group 2.

[6] Meteyard, *Life*, II, p. 593.

[7] *Ibid.*, II, pp. 593 ff.

[8] R. E. Raspe, *Catalogue Raisonné d'une Collection Générale de Pierres Gravés Antiques et Modernes*, II, p. 542, nos. 9285, 9289.

[9] Hautecoeur, *op. cit.*, p. 219.

[10] Carl Robert, *Die Antiken Sarkophag-Reliefs*, II, p. 45.

[11] Zoega, App. Fol. 125, quoted in Robert, *op. cit.*, II, p. 45.

[12] Meteyard, *Life*, II, p. 592.

[13] Jones, *Museo Capitolino*, p. 78.

[14] *Ibid.*, Pl. 16; Pietro Santi Bartoli and Giovanni Pietro Bellori, *Veterum Sepulcra*, Pls. 81–83; Righetti, *op. cit.*, Pls. 137–139; Bernard de Montfaucon, *Antiquité Expliquée*, V, 1, Pl. XCI.

[15] Jones, *Museo Capitolino*, p. 80.

[16] *Ibid.*, p. 81.

[17] *Ibid.*, p. 78.

[18] *Ibid.*, p. 80.

[19] *Ibid.*, p. 80.

[20] Georg Lippold, *Gemmen und Kameen des Altertums und der Neuzeit*, Pl. CXLII, no. 2; Raspe, *op. cit.*, no. 9302.

[21] Robert, *op. cit.*, II, Pls. XVI–XVII.

[22] John Swarbrick, *Robert Adam and His Brothers*, p. 266, Fig. 201.

[23] Emil Hannover, "Europe and Near East; Earthenware and Stoneware," *Pottery and Porcelain*, I, p. 530 (tr. by B. Rackham).

[24] Jones, *Museo Capitolino*, p. 78.

[25] Gives source as the carnelian but discusses the rock crystal.

[26] Raspe, *op. cit.*, no. 13829, II, Pl. LVII.

[27] French *Catalogue,* 1788, Class I, Section I, no. 585, "standing with a serpent, cornelian (*sic*)."

[28] Reinach, *Répertoire de Reliefs,* III, p. 181, no. 3; Jones, *Museo Capitolino,* Pl. 63.

[29] Jones, *Museo Capitolino,* p. 267.

[30] John D. Beazley, *Attic Red-figure Vase-Painters,* p. 964.

[31] Montfaucon, *op. cit.,* I, 1, Pl. XLII, no. 3; Raspe, *op. cit.,* no. 2941; I, p. 206.

[32] M. H. Nevil Story-Maskelyne, *The Marlborough Gems,* no. 344.

[33] Adolf Furtwängler, *Die Antiken Gemmen,* II, p. 300, illustrated *ibid.,* I, Pl. LXV, no. 21.

[34] Story-Maskelyne, *op. cit.,* p. 61.

[35] Furtwängler, *op. cit.,* II, p. 300.

[36] T. Worlidge, *A Select Collection of Drawings from Curious Antique Gems,* no. 37.

[37] Anne Claude Philippe, Comte de Caylus, *Recueil d'Antiquités Egyptiennes, Etrusques, Grecques et Romaines,* V. Pl. LIII, no. 3.

[38] Worlidge, *op. cit.,* no. 57.

[39] *Gemmarum Antiquarum Expraestantionibus Desumptus, quae in Dactylioth Ducis Marlburiensis Conservantur,* I, Pl. XLVI.

[40] Sir William Hamilton and P. H. d'Hancarville, *Antiquités Etrusques, Grecques et Romaines,* I, Pl. 129.

[41] Cecil Smith, *Catalogue of the Greek and Etruscan Vases in the British Museum,* III, *Vases of the Finest Period,* no. E 224; Joseph C. Hoppin, *A Handbook of Attic Red-figured Vases, Vol. II,* pp. 177 ff.

[42] Hamilton and d'Hancarville, *op. cit.,* I, Pl. 127.

[43] P. J. Mariette, *Traité des Pierres Gravées et un Recueil des Pierres Gravées du Cabinet du Roy,* II, Pl. XLI.

[44] Baumeister, *op. cit.,* II, p. 848, classifies the figure as a maenad; Pierre Bouillon and J. B. de Saint-Victor, *Musée des Antiques,* I (Bas-reliefs); Reinach, *Répertoire de la Statuaire Grècque et Romaine,* I, p. 32.

[45] E. Q. Visconti and Comte de Clarac, *Description des Antiques du Musée Royale,* no. 200, classifies it as a maenad.

[46] Meteyard, *Life,* II, pp. 363 ff.

[47] W. G. Constable, *John Flaxman,* Appendix I, p. 82, list of accredited work for Wedgwood.

[48] Meteyard, *Life,* II, p. 364.

[49] Hamilton and d'Hancarville, *op. cit.,* 1801–1808 ed., III, Pl. 31; Smith, *op. cit.,* no. E 460.

[50] Mariette, *op. cit.,* II, Pl. XXXI.

[51] Arthur T. Bolton, *The Architecture of Robert and James Adam,* I, p. 263.

[52] Lippold, *Gemmen,* Pl. XLII, no. 11; Furtwängler, *op. cit.,* Pl. XLIX, no. 2.

[53] Lippold, *Gemmen,* Pl. XLII, no. 1; Furtwängler, *op. cit.,* pl. XLIX, no. 1.

[54] Erasmo Pistolesi, *Reale Museo Borbonico,* I, p. 294, Pl. LXIV.

[55] For discussion of the origin of the composition of the Diomedes gem type

see A. Conze, "Das Vorbild der Diomedes-Gemmen," *Jahrbuch*, IV, 1889, pp. 87–90.

[56] C. O. Müller, *Ancient Art and Its Remains* (new ed. by F. G. Welcker, tr. by John Leitch), p. 489.

[57] Guigniaut, *op. cit.*, no. 436; Montfaucon, *op. cit.*, I, 2, Pl. CXLII, no. 1; Pistolesi, *Museo Borbonico*, IV, Pl. XXXVII; Reinach, *Répertoire de Reliefs*, III, p. 69; Baumeister, *op. cit.*, I, p. 438.

[58] Smith, *op. cit.*, III, p. 700.

[59] Montfaucon, *op. cit.*, III, 2, Pl. CXXXIV, in the Cabinet de Bourdaloüe.

[60] Mariette, *op. cit.*, II, Pl. XLVII.

[61] Jones, *Museo Capitolino*, Pl. 24; Reinach, *Répertoire de Reliefs*, III, p. 183, no. 6; Righetti, *op. cit.*, I, Pl. 161.

[62] Jones, *Museo Capitolino*, p. 119.

[63] Reinach, *Répertoire de Reliefs*, III, p. 68.

[64] Heinrich Bulle, *Der Schöne Mensch im Altertum*, p. 68, Pl. 189.

[65] Raphael Gargiulo, *Collection of the Most Remarkable Objects of the National Museum*, I, Pl. 46.

[66] Bulle, *op. cit.*, p. 62.

[67] Reinach, *Répertoire de Reliefs*, I, p. 14; Baumeister, *op. cit.*, II, p. 841; Roscher, *op. cit.*, IV, pp. 481–482; Guigniaut, *op. cit.*, no. 446.

[68] Bolton, *op. cit.*, I, p. 117.

[69] *Catalogue Sommaire des Marbres Antiques du Louvre*, Pl. V; Roscher, *op. cit.*, II, 2, 2271; *Sculture del Palazzo della Villa Borghese*, I, Stanza II, no. 10; Pietro Santi Bartoli and Giovanni Pietro Bellori, *Admiranda Romanarum Antiquitatum ac Veteris Sculpturae Vestigia*, Pls. 50–51; Guigniaut, *op. cit.*, no. 479; Montfaucon, *op. cit.*, II, 1, Pl. LXXXVI.

[70] Bouillon and Saint-Victor, *op. cit.*, I, no. 2 (bas-reliefs).

[71] Pistolesi, *Museo Borbonico*, II, Pl. V; Gargiulo, *op. cit.*, III, Pl. 39; Reinach, *Répertoire de Peintures Grecques et Romaines*, p. 345, no. 3; Wolfgang Helbig, *Wandgemälde der vom Vesuv Verschütteten Städte Campaniens*, no. 500.

[72] Righetti, *op. cit.*, I, Pl. XVI; Jones, *Museo Capitolino*, Pl. 53.

[73] Jones, *Museo Capitolino*, p. 219.

[74] Furtwängler, *op. cit.*, I, Pl. LVII, no. 11; *Gem. Ant. Marlb.*, I, Pl. L; Philippe de Stosch, *Pierres Antiques Gravées*, Pl. LXX; Guigniaut, *op. cit.*, no. 408; Montfaucon, *op. cit.*, I, 1, Pl. CXXI, no. 1; Raspe, *op. cit.*, no. 7199, I, p. 417.

[75] Story-Maskelyne, *op. cit.*, p. xxvii.

[76] *Ibid.*, p. 27.

[77] *Ibid.*, p. 26.

[78] Roux and Barré, *op. cit.*, II, p. 75, Pl. 19; Georges Méautis, *Chefs d'Oeuvre de la Peinture Grecque*, Pl. 32; Guigniaut, *op. cit.*, no. 404; Pistolesi, *Museo Borbonico*, IV, Pl. XIII; G. E. Rizzo, *La Pittura Ellenistico-Romana*, Pl. CXXXVIII; Reinach, *Répertoire de Peintures*, p. 77, no. 3.

[79] M. Brown, *French Painting of the Revolution*, p. 74, Pl. II; also discussed

and illustrated in André Michel, *Histoire de l'Art depuis Les Premiers Temps Chrétiens jusqu'à Nos Jours*, VII, p. 543.

80 M. Praz, "Herculaneum and European Taste," *Magazine of Art*, XXXII, 1939, p. 690, ill. p. 686.

81 Lippold, *Gemmen*, Pl. CXXIII, no. 13.

82 P. A. Maffei and D. de Rossi, *Gemme Antiche Figurate*, IV, 74, has the title "La Virtu ridatta in Servitu dal Vizio"; Montfaucon, *op. cit.*, I, 1, Pl. CXXII, no. 3.

83 Antonio Francisco Gori, *Museum Florentinum, Gemmae Antiquae*, II, Pl. I, no. 1; Joseph Spence, *Polymetis*, Pl. VII, no. 1; Montfaucon, *op. cit.*, I, 1, Pl. CXV, no. 2; Furtwängler, *op. cit.*, I, Pl. LVII, no. 1.

84 Agostini, *op. cit.*, I, Pl. 116; Maffei and De Rossi, *Gemme Antiche*, III, Pl. 3; Montfaucon, *op. cit.*, I, 1, Pl. CV, no. 1.

85 Robert and James Adam, *The Decorative Work: Being a Reproduction of the Plates Illustrating Decoration and Furniture from Works in Architecture*, 1778–1812, Pl. XXII.

86 Robert, *op. cit.*, III, 1, Pl. XII, no. 40; Jones, *Museo Capitolino*, Pl. 35, pp. 152 ff.; Righetti, *op. cit.*, I, Pl. CXL.

87 Jones, *Museo Capitolino*, Pl. 26; Pierre Gusman, *L'Art Decoratif de Rome*, I, Pl. 34; Righetti, *op. cit.*, I, Pl. CLX; Eugenie Strong, *Roman Sculpture*, II, p. 266, Pl. 80.

88 Jones, *Museo Capitolino*, p. 91.

89 Jones, *Museo Capitolino*, Pl. 83, pp. 331 ff.; Righetti, *op. cit.*, I, Pl. CIX; Guigniaut, *op. cit.*, no. 251.

90 Jones, *Museo Capitolino*, p. 332.

91 Pistolesi, *Museo Borbonico*, I. Pl. XCVI.

92 François Perrier, *Segmanta Nobilium Signorum e Statuarii . . .* , Pl. 62.

93 Bartoli and Bellori, *Admiranda*, Pl. 59; Montfaucon, *op. cit.*, III, Pl. CXXXII, no. 1; Reinach, *Répertoire de la Statuaire*, I, p. 91.

94 Robert and James Adam, *The Decorative Work*, Pl. V; Adam, *Works in Architecture*, Pl. VI, Syon House; Bolton, *op. cit.*, I, Pl. 256.

95 Bolton, *op. cit.*, II, p. 231.

96 Walters, *Vases of the Latest Period*, IV, p. 239, no. G 19.

97 Hamilton and d'Hancarville, *op. cit.*, II, Pl. 94.

98 Lippold, *Gemmen*, Pl. CXXXI, no. 4.

99 Reinach, *Répertoire de Peintures*, p. 158, no. 4.

100 Roux and Barré, *op. cit.*, IV, p. 102; Pl. 36; Gargiulo, *op. cit.*, III, Pl. 47; Pistolesi, *Museo Borbonico*, V, Pl. LXII; Reinach, *Répertoire de Peintures*, p. 136, no. 6.

101 Helbig, *op. cit.*, no. 1937.

102 Helbig, *op. cit.*, no. 1921, illustrated in Pistolesi, *Museo Borbonico*, V. Pl. LXIII, and Roux and Barré, *op. cit.*, IV, p. 77, Pl. 27, called "Peace."

103 Roux and Barré, *op. cit.*, IV, p. 107, Pl. 37; Pistolesi, *Museo Borbonico*, V, Pl. LXIII; Gargiulo, *op. cit.*, III, Pl. 48; Reinach, *Répertoire de Peintures*, p. 133, no. 5.

104 Helbig, *op. cit.,* no. 1928.

105 Adam, *Decorative Work,* Pl. XXVI, *Works in Architecture,* I, Pl. VII, of Queen's House.

106 Pirro Marconi, *La Pittura dei Romani,* Pl. 34.

107 Roux and Barré, *op. cit.,* IV, p. 81, Pl. 28; Pistolesi, *Museo Borbonico,* V, Pl. LXV; Gargiulo, *op. cit.,* III, Pl. 50; Reinach, *Répertoire de Peintures,* p. 136, no. 10.

108 Helbig, *op. cit.,* no. 1923.

109 Roux and Barré, *op. cit.,* IV, p. 161, Pl. 161; Pistolesi, *Museo Borbonico,* II, Pl. VI; Gargiulo, *op. cit.,* II, Pl. 39; Praz, *loc. cit.,* p. 691; Reinach, *Répertoire de Peintures,* p. 345, no. 5.

110 Helbig, *op. cit.,* no. 502.

111 Méautis, *op. cit.,* Fig. 24; Roux and Barré, *op. cit.,* II, p. 149, Pl. 45; Pistolesi, *Museo Borbonico,* I, Pl. XVI; Guigniaut, *op. cit.,* no. 843; Reinach, *Répertoire de Peintures,* p. 172, no. 3.

112 Helbig, *op. cit.,* no. 1048.

113 Reinach, *Répertoire de Peintures,* p. 124, no. 5; Roux and Barré, *op. cit.,* II, p. 9.

114 Helbig, *op. cit.,* nos. 451, 589.

115 Praz, *loc. cit.,* discusses the use of such motifs in palaces and private homes.

116 H. Stuart Jones, "Provenance of the Portland Vase," *Athenaeum,* Feb. 27, 1909, p. 265. This point cannot be too emphatically made as the baseless story of the finding of the Barberini or Portland Vase in the sarcophagus found on the Monte del Grano has been repeated since Bartoli and Bellori's *Veterum Sepulcra* appeared at the end of the seventeenth century. Jones recapitulates the history of the vase and disproves Bartoli and Bellori.

117 Jones, *Museo Capitolino,* Pl. 63; Robert, *op. cit.,* III, 2, Pl. XCVII, no. 293, p. 353; Righetti, *op. cit.,* I, Pl. 171.

118 Jones, *Museo Capitolino,* p. 268.

119 Bolton, *op. cit.,* I, p. 33.

120 Strong, *op. cit.,* Pl. XIII.

121 Raspe, *op. cit.,* II, p. 615, no. 10746, a composition of four figures on a carnelian belonging to a Mr. Nicol.

122 Agostini, *op. cit.,* II, no. 23; Montfaucon, *op. cit.,* II, 1, Pl. XCIV, no. 14; Maffei and De Rossi, *Gemme Antiche,* IV, Pl. 9.

123 Montfaucon, *op. cit.,* I, 1, Pl. LIX, no. 1; *Catalogue Sommaire des Marbres du Louvre,* Pl. LIII; Righetti, *op. cit.,* I, Pl. XCII; Bouillon and Saint-Victor, *op. cit.,* III (bas-reliefs); Roscher, *op. cit.,* II, 2, 3273–4; Ch. Daremberg, Edm. Saglio, Edm. Pottier, *Dictionnaire des Antiquités Grècques et Romaines,* VI, p. 2068; Reinach, *Répertoire de la Statuaire,* I, p. 93.

124 Swarbrick, *op. cit.,* p. 267, fig. 201.

125 Lippold, *Gemmen,* Pl. CXXXIII, no. 12; impressions no. 472–474 of Thomas A. Boggs Collection of Tassie Impressions in the Walters Art Gallery, Baltimore, Md.; Raspe, *op. cit.,* I, p. 336.

126 Boggs Collection of Tassie Impressions, drawer CCC, no. 3207.

127 Raspe, *op. cit.*, no. 8108, I, p. 474, Pl. XLVIII, signed by Pichler.

128 Lippold, *Gemmen*, Pl. CXXXIII, no. 9.

129 Roux and Barré, *op. cit.*, IV, p. 14, Pl. 4; Guigniaut, *op. cit.*, no. 290; Reinach, *Répertoire de Peintures*, p. 153, no. 2; Reinach, *Répertoire de la Statuaire*, I, p. 268.

130 Helbig, *op. cit.*, no. 871.

131 Bolton, *op. cit.*, II, p. 211.

132 Helbig, *op. cit.*, no. 878; Reinach, *Répertoire de Peintures*, p. 153, no. 1; Reinach, *Répertoire de la Statuaire*, I. p. 256; Roscher, *op. cit.*, II, 2, p. 3273; Guigniaut, *op. cit.*, no. 291; Roux and Barré, *op. cit.*, IV, p. 19, Pl. 5.

133 Raspe, *op. cit.*, p. 336, no. 3502; Boggs Collection of Tassie Impressions, no. 469, drawer H.

134 Hautecoeur, *op. cit.*, p. 219.

135 H. A. Grueber, *Coins of the Roman Republic in the British Museum*, III, Pl. XLV, no. 17.

136 Lippold, *Gemmen*, Pl. CXXXIII, no. 7; Raspe, *op. cit.*, I, p. 337, no. 3504; Boggs Collection of Tassie Impressions, no. 478, drawer H.

137 Lippold, *Gemmen*, Pl. LIX, no. 2; Furtwängler, *op. cit.*, I, Pl. XXXV, no. 23; Gori, *op. cit.*, II, Pl. 4; de Stosch, *op. cit.*, Pl. XLV; Raspe, *op. cit.*, no. 3440; Agostini, *op. cit.*, II, 10.

138 De Stosch, *op. cit.*, p. 9, in discussion of the same subject in the Strozzi collection.

139 Lippold, *Gemmen*, Pl. CXXXIII, no. 10; Raspe, *op. cit.*, no. 3441.

140 Raspe, *op. cit.*, I, A 234; Boggs Collection of Tassie Impressions, nos. 461–466.

141 De Stosch, *op. cit.*, Pl. VII.

142 Raspe, *op. cit.*, no. 3444, an emerald.

143 Furtwängler, *op. cit.*, II, p. 171.

144 O. M. Dalton, *Catalogue of Engraved Gems of the Post-classical Periods . . . in the British Museum*, nos. 780–781.

145 Grueber, *op. cit.*, III, Pl. XLV, no. 14; Montfaucon, *op. cit.*, I, 1, Pl. LIX, same series nos. 2–11.

146 *Sculture della Villa Borghese*, I, Stanza I, no. 14; Reinach, *Répertoire de la Statuaire*, I, p. 58.

147 Righetti, *op. cit.*, II, Pl. CCXXV; Bartoli and Bellori, *Admiranda*, Pls. 31, 32; Montfaucon, *op. cit.*, I, 1, Pl. C; Bouillon and Saint-Victor, *op. cit.*, I (bas-reliefs); Reinach, *Répertoire de la Statuaire*, I, p. 94; Guigniaut, *op. cit.*, no. 511; Visconti and Clarac, *op. cit.*, no. 75.

148 Bartoli, Bellori, and La Chausse, *Picturae Antiquae*, Pl. IX; Reinach, *Répertoire de Peintures*, p. 140, no. 8.

149 Bartoli, Bellori, and La Chausse, *Picturae Antiquae*, Pl. VII; Reinach, *Répertoire de Peintures*, p. 148, no. 11.

150 B. Rackham, *English Porcelain in the Victoria and Albert Museum*, no. 116, Pl. 30.

151 *Ibid.*, no. 365, Pl. 65.

152 Lippold, *Gemmen*, Pl. CXI, no. 7.

[153] Robert, *op. cit.*, II, Pl. LVII, Nos. 167, 167a, 167b, p. 177; Winckelmann, *Monumenti Antichi Inediti,* I, fig. 149; Roscher, *op. cit.,* III, 1, p. 1002; Guigniaut, *op. cit.,* no. 839.

[154] Robert, *op. cit.,* II, p. 177.

[155] Robert, *op. cit.,* II, Pl. IV, 10, 10′, 10″; Roscher, *op. cit.,* III¹, pp. 1621, 1622; D. Raoul-Rochette, *Monumens Inedits d'Antiquité Grecque, Etrusque, et Romaine,* Pl. L, 1; Reinach, *Répertoire de Reliefs,* II, p. 246, no. 2.

[156] Pistolesi, *Museo Borbonico,* II, p. 90.

[157] Pistolesi, *Museo Borbonico,* II, Pl. XXII; Reinach, *Répertoire de Reliefs,* II, p. 80, no. 4; Gargiulo, *op. cit.,* I, 47; Winckelmann, *Monumenti Antichi Inediti,* I, fig. 115; Guigniaut, *op. cit.,* no. 752.

[158] A. J. B. Wace, "The Reliefs in the Palazzo Spada," *Papers of the British School at Rome,* V, Pl. XX, Fig. 1; Baumeister, *op. cit.,* I, p. 300; Guigniaut, *op. cit.,* no. 615.

[159] Wace, *loc. cit.,* pp. 186 ff.

[160] Reinach, *Répertoire de Peintures,* p. 181, no. 2; Guigniaut, *op. cit.,* no. 619.

[161] Michaelis, "Das Grabmal des Nasonier," *Jahrbuch,* XXV, 1910, pp. 101 ff., gives plates from Bartoli and Bellori and discusses various editions the work has seen.

[162] R. P. Hinks, *Catalogue of the Greek, Etruscan, and Roman Paintings and Mosaics in the British Museum,* p. 48.

[163] Jones, *Museo Capitolino,* Pl. 53; Bartoli and Bellori, *Admiranda,* Pl. 34; Righetti, *op. cit.,* I, Pl. LXXII; Guigniaut, *op. cit.,* no. 613; Roscher, *op. cit.,* I, p. 346.

[164] Lippold, *Gemmen,* Pl. CXLIV, no. 6. Signed by (L.) Pichler.

[165] Raspe, *op. cit.,* II, p. 522, no. 8880. Rock crystal. From an antique bas-relief in the Capitol. Signed by Pichler.

[166] Jones, *Museo Capitolino,* p. 219.

[167] Swarbrick, *op. cit.,* p. 146, Fig. 104; Adam, *Works in Architecture,* I, Pl. VI, Syon House.

[168] Jones, *Museo Capitolino,* Pl. 65, pp. 180 ff.; Righetti, *op. cit.,* I, Pl. LXXIII, LXXIV; Winckelmann, *Monumenti Antichi Inediti,* I, Fig. 5.

[169] Walther Amelung, *Die Sculpturen des Vaticanischen Museums,* II, Pl. 7, pp. 142–145; Pistolesi, *Il Vaticano,* IV, Pl. CVIII; Bartoli and Bellori, *Admiranda,* Pl. 16; Montfaucon, *op. cit.,* II, 2, Pl. CXVI, no. 1.

[170] Strong, *op. cit.,* pp. 40 ff.

[171] Reinach, *Répertoire de la Statuaire,* I, p. 112; Winckelmann, *Monumenti Antichi Inediti,* I, Fig. 120.

[172] Visconti et Clarac, *op. cit.,* I, no. 175.

[173] Montfaucon, *op. cit.,* II, 1, Pl. XCII, no. 4; Dalton, *op. cit.,* Pl. XXX, no. 833; Lippold, *Gemmen,* Pl. CXLIX, no. 3; Furtwängler, *op. cit.,* I, Pl. LXVII, no. 23, a paste copy in Munich.

[174] Swarbrick, *op. cit.,* p. 272, Fig. 206.

[175] *Ibid.,* p. 15, Fig. 10; Bolton, *op. cit.,* I, Frontispiece.

[176] Mariette, *op. cit.,* II, Pl. LXVII; Raspe, *op. cit.,* II, p. 681, no. 12689, a carnelian, also under "unknown subject."

[177] Amelung, *op. cit.*, II, Pls. 60 (Zeus) and 61 (Hera); Reinach, *Répertoire de Reliefs*, III, p. 396; Pistolesi, *Il Vaticano*, V, Pl. XXX.

[178] Amelung, *op. cit.*, II, p. 633.

[179] Lippold, *Gemmen*, Pl. CXVI, no. 4.

V

Conclusion

———

A CROSS SECTION OF THE CLASSIC DESIGNS USED ON WEDG-
wood pottery has been studied in an attempt to discover and
compare the sources and their pottery interpretations. The ideas
and trends which determined the selection of these motifs for
ceramic adaptation have also been discussed.

Wedgwood's utilization of Greek, Hellenistic, and Roman designs is apparent and unquestioned. The actual source materials
were original *objets d'art,* casts, gems, books, and prints. The originals were obtained through access to the private collections so
numerous among the English nobility of that period. The most
famous antique from which the potter worked directly was the
Portland Vase. Others were from cabinets of engraved gems belonging to the Duke of Marlborough, Sir Watkin Williams
Wynne, and others. Casts of ancient monuments came from deal-
ers such as the elder Flaxman and also through the agency of
Thomas Jenkins, who handled Wedgwood's business in Rome.
Casts of sarcophagi, altars, free-standing statues, and gems modelled by local artists such as Pacetti and Dalmazzoni were sent to
England. They came from the great private collections of Italy
and from the Vatican and Capitoline Museums. Often damaged,

the originals were freely restored. Flaxman, too, went to Rome to study and there modelled from the antique for Wedgwood.

A most important source for impressions of gems was a competitor, James Tassie, who had made his reproductions in wax and paste before Wedgwood entered the field. The latter's first pottery cameos were obtained from casts bought from Tassie. Plates in books supplied the inspiration for many Wedgwood designs. These books were owned by the firm of Wedgwood and Bentley, were loaned or presented to the firm for study, or were used in the British Museum. The inventory of books owned by the firm has been discussed. Archaeological treatises of the time were prone to illustrate the antique with a very free interpretation, hence pottery designs copied from such prints were often far removed from the original ancient work.

The adaptations of classical motifs can be classified as follows:

(1) Classic works used with no change except in drapery. These are exemplified by *Orestes and Pylades,* the *Crowning of a Citharist,* and the *Judgment of Paris,* among others.

(2) Classic works used in part with some figures changed, for example, the *Birth of Dionysus.* In this group belong the so-called "composition pieces" consisting of figures taken separately from widely varying sources (as in several of the *Sacrifices*) and also those works which derive from badly damaged ancient pieces and which were freely restored by the artists employed by the potter, for example, *Death of a Roman Warrior.*

(3) Works copied from ancient art and recopied by Wedgwood through an intermediary source, as in the case of the casts of gems purchased from James Tassie and in the designs derived from prints and books. In these pieces the motifs are frequently so far removed from the ancient source that the latter is virtually unrecognizable.

(4) Works classic in manner but of Renaissance or later workmanship, for example, the late Renaissance works, the "Cachet of Michelangelo" and the *Marriage of Cupid and Psyche* and the eighteenth-century *Priapus Decorated by Nymphs* from an original by Angelica Kauffman.

Wedgwood's designs on the whole reflect the three basic and sometimes overlapping artistic trends of the eighteenth century, the Rococo, Neoclassicism, and moralizing sentimentalism, even though Wedgwood was convinced that he was in the vanguard of the revival of the classic and the revolt against the ornate Rococo style. His motifs mirror the survival of the Rococo in such designs as *Venus in Her Chariot* by Vigée-Lebrun and even of the late Baroque in the extensive use of the small, lively boys of Il Fiammingo and the works of Giovanni da Bologna. Besides the strong classical trend, there is seen the later moralizing, sentimental tendency which was a grim combination of the philosophy of Rousseau, the artistic ideals of Diderot and the painting of Greuze, for example, the designs of Miss Crewe entitled *Maternal Love, Infancy*, etc.

The fundamental reason, however, for the selection of so many classical designs was economic rather than sentimental. The study of ancient art may have been and probably was a sincere interest of Wedgwood. But his sincerity was undoubtedly modified by the fact that the ceramic-artist was also a manufacturer who wished to offer objects for sale to a remunerative market. Classicism was a great golden wave for the art-craftsmen of this period, and Josiah Wedgwood rode its crest. The potter's interest in the customer is amusingly illustrated in his "censoring" of antique originals for pottery adaptation. If, for example, the nudity of the figures repelled his public, he covered the nudity. The more earthy elements of the earlier civilization, ever present in its art, are completely bypassed. The potter considered he was "improving" ancient art in suiting it to the tastes of his customers. Professor George Boas' comment upon the use of the classic in the eighteenth century is most appropriate in this regard: [1] "The Greek heroes and gods, as depicted by the vase-painters [sixth to fourth centuries B.C.] are not the 'aesthetic,' somewhat wan, and always graceful personages of the neoclassic artists. They are robust, vigorous and usually animal beings drawn with a vivacity which only folk-painters or caricaturists achieve today. They are not spiritualized nor prettified. They are frequently represented with

a realism which would be considered obscene even by the liber-
ated public of our day. When one compares them with the figures
on Wedgwood pieces, one realizes the tremendous gap between
their point of view and ours; one becomes more acutely aware
than ever before of how little like the real Greeks our Greeks are,
how each age creates its own Greeks."

There is no doubt that the potter employed an extensive reper-
toire of Greek and Roman motifs. His choice of particular subjects, however, was indiscriminate, and his evaluation of their
artistic merit is open to criticism. He changed and combined im-
partially the good, mediocre, and bad examples of Greco-Roman
art with those of the Renaissance and his own day. Wedgwood
cannot, therefore, be called an innovator in the history of art and
a "spreader of the gospel of the antique."

The true value, then, of Josiah Wedgwood and his productions
lies not in his use of classical motifs upon his pottery; it lies in the
pottery itself. He was a great empiric chemist who invented new
bodies and improved old ones; and it is in this field that his true
merit rests. This view of the matter is well summarized by the
Rheads in their comment on the artistic merits of Josiah Wedgwood: [2] "Wedgwood's style, so far from being 'strikingly original'
was the prevailing style of the period, a quasi-classicism, not by
any means admirable, but still good of its kind. . . . The brothers
Adam had far more to do with influencing artistic taste than
Wedgwood, who did not influence it in the least, but simply accepted existing conditions. We are still waiting for the man who
will inaugurate a new art epoch and make a fortune at the same
time." Wedgwood "accepted existing conditions" enthusiastically,
for when he died he left a fortune of half a million pounds.

[1] George Boas, "The Greek Tradition in Painting," *The Greek Tradition in
Painting and the Minor Arts,* An Exhibition Sponsored . . . by the Baltimore Museum of Art and the Walters Art Gallery, 1939, p. 1.

[2] G. W. Rhead and F. A. Rhead, *Staffordshire Pots and Potters,* pp. 224 ff.

Bibliography

Adam, Robert and James. *The Decorative Work: Being a Reproduction of the Plates Illustrating Decoration and Furniture from Works in Architecture, 1778–1812.* London, 1901, Batsford.

Agostini, Lionardo. *Gemmae et Sculpturae Antiquae . . .* , Addita earum enarratione in Latinum versa ab Jacobo Gronovio . . . Amsterdam, 1685, Abraham Blooteling.

Amelung, Walther. *Die Sculpturen des Vaticanischen Museums.* Berlin, 1903–1908, Reimer.

Arnaud, Francois, and Henri Coquille. *Description des Principales Pierres Gravées du Cabinet de S. A. S. Monseigneur le Duc d'Orléans.* 2 vols. Paris, 1780–1784, La Chau.

Ashby, Thomas. "Thomas Jenkins in Rome," *Papers of the British School at Rome,* VI, no. 8, pp. 487–511. London, 1913.

Babelon, Ernest. *Histoire de la Gravure sur Gemmes en France.* Paris, 1902.

Bagrani, Gilbert, "Winckelmann and the Second Renascence," *American Journal of Archaeology,* LIX, p. 107 ff.

Barnard, Harry. *Chats on Wedgwood Ware.* New York, 1924, Frederick A. Stokes.

Bartoli, Pietro Santi. *Museum Odeschalchum sive Thesaurus Antiquarum Gemmarum.* 2 vols. Rome, 1751–1752, Monaldini.

Bartoli, Pietro Santi, and Giovanni Pietro Bellori. *Admiranda Romanarum Antiquitatum ac Veteris Sculpturae Vestigia.* Rome, 1693.

———. *Le Antiche Lucerne Sepolcrali Figurate.* Rome, 1691.

———. *Veterum Sepulcra.* Rome, 1728.

Bartoli, Pietro Santi, Francisco Bartoli, Giovanni Pietro Bellori, and Michelange de la Chausse. *Picturae Antiquae, Cryptarum Romanarum, et Sepulcri Nasonum.* 3 parts. Rome, 1750.

Baumeister, August. *Denkmäler des Klassischen Altertums.* 3 vols. Leipzig, 1885–1888. R. Oldenbourg.

Beazley, John D. *Attic Red-figure Vase Painters.* Oxford, 1942, Clarenden Press.

Bieber, Margarete. *Laocoon.* New York, 1942, Columbia University Press.

Biographie Universelle, nouvelle ed., M. Michaud, ed. 45 vols. Paris, 1854–1865, Mme. C. Desplaces.

Blacker, J. F., *Nineteenth Century English Ceramic Art.* London, n.d., Stanley Paul.

Boas, George. "The Greek Tradition in Painting," *The Greek Tradition,* Exhibition Sponsored by the Baltimore Museum of Art and the Walters Art Gallery from May 15 through June 25, 1939.

Bolton, Arthur T. *The Architecture of Robert and James Adam.* 2 vols. London, 1922, George Newnes.

Bouillon, Pierre, and J. B. de Saint-Victor. *Musée des Antiques.* 3 vols. Paris, n.d., P. Didot.

Bulle, Heinrich. *Der Schöne Mensch im Altertum.* Munich and Leipzig, 1898, Hirth.

Burton, William. *History and Description of English Earthenware and Stoneware.* London, 1904, Cassell.

Catalogue of the Very Celebrated Collection of Antique Gems of the Prince Poniatowski deceased; . . . sold . . . by Messrs. Christie and Manson. London, 1839, Clowes and Sons.

Caylus, Anne Claude Philippe, Comte de. *Recueil d'Antiquités Egyptiennes, Etrusques, Grecques et Romaines.* 8 vols. Paris, 1756–1770, Desaint and Saillant.

Church, Sir Arthur Herbert. *English Earthenware,* South Kensington Museum Art Handbook. London, 1884.

———. *Josiah Wedgwood, Master-Potter,* Portfolio Artistic Monographs, no. 3. London, 1894, Seeley and Company.

Constable, W. G., *John Flaxman.* London, 1927, University of London Press.

Conze, Alexander. "Das Vorbild der Diomedes-Gemmen," *Jahrbuch des Kaiserlich Deutschen Archäologischen Instituts,* IV, 1889, pp. 87–90.

Dagley, Richard. *Gems Selected from the Antique.* London, 1804, John Murray.

Dalton, Ormonde M. *Catalogue of the Ivory Carvings of the Christian Era in the British Museum.* London, 1909.

———. *Catalogue of Engraved Gems of the Post-classical Periods in the British Museum.* London, 1915.

Daremberg, Ch., Edm. Saglio, and Edm. Pottier. *Dictionnaire des Antiquités Grecques et Romaines.* Paris, 1904, Librarie Hachette.

De la Beche, Henry. *Catalogue of Specimens in the Museum of Practical Geology . . .* 2nd ed. by T. Reeks and F. W. Rudler. London, 1871, George E. Eyre.

De la Fosse, Jean Charles. *Nouvelle Iconologie Historique.* Paris, 1771, J. F. Chereau.

Description of the Collection of Ancient Marbles in the British Museum. London, 1812, W. Nicol.

Description of the Collection of Ancient Terra Cottas in the British Museum. London, 1810, W. Bulmer and Company.

Ducati, Pericle. *L'Arte in Roma dalle Origini al Secolo VIII.* Bologna, 1938, Capelli.

Eckhel, Abbé. *Choix des Pierres Gravées du Cabinet Impérial des Antiques.* Vienna, 1788, Joseph Noble de Kurzbek.

Ficoroni, Francisco. *Gemmae Antiquae Litteratae.* Rome, 1757, Monaldini.

Fortnum, C. Drury. "Notes on Some of the Antique and Renaissance Gems and Jewels . . . at Windsor Castle," *Archaeologia,* XLV, 1877, pp. 1–28.

Furtwängler, Adolf. *Die Antiken Gemmen.* 3 vols. Leipzig and Berlin, 1900, Giesicke and Devrient.

Gardner, Ernest Arthur. *Handbook of Greek Sculpture.* 2nd ed. London, 1915, Macmillan.

Gargiulo, Raphael. *Collection of the Most Remarkable Monuments of the National Museum.* 4 vols. Naples, 1872.

Gatty, Charles T. *Catalogue of a Loan Collection of the Works of Josiah Wedgwood.* Liverpool, 1879, Liverpool Art Club.

Gemmarum Antiquarum Expraestantionibus Desumptus, quae in Dactyliothecis Ducis Marburiensis Conservantur. 2 vols. London, 1845, J. Murray.

Gorely, Jean, ed. *Old Wedgwood,* Old Wedgwood Club. Wellesley Press, 1938, 1939, 1941.

Gorely, Jean, and Mary Wadsworth. *Exhibition Catalogue of Old Wedgwood from the Bequest of Grenville Lindall Winthrop,* Fogg Museum of Art, Harvard University, 1944.

Gori, Antonio Francisco. *Gemmae Antiquae, Museum Florentinum,* I, II. Florence, 1731.

Graham, John Meredith and Hensleigh Cecil Wedgwood. *Wedgwood.* Brooklyn Institute of Fine Arts, 1948, Brooklyn Museum.

Grant, Maurice Harold. *Makers of Black Basaltes.* London, 1910, William Blackwood.

Grueber, H. A. *Coins of the Roman Republic in the British Museum.* 3 vols. London, 1910.

Guattani, G. *Monumenti Antichi Inediti.* Rome, 1784–1879, Pagliarini.

Guigniaut, J. D. *Nouvelle Galérie Mythologique Comprenant la Galerie Mythologique de feu A. L. Millin.* Paris, 1850.

Gusman, Pierre. *L'Art Décoratif de Rome de la Fin de la République au IVe Siècle.* Paris, 1908?, Maison Morel, Ch. Eggimann.

———. *La Villa d'Hadrien près de Tivoli.* Paris, 1908, Hachette.

Hamilton, Sir William, and P. H. d'Hancarville. *Antiquités Etrusques, Grecques et Romaines.* 4 vols. Naples, 1766–1767. 2nd ed. 1801–1808.

Hamilton, Sir William. *Collection of Engravings from Ancient Vases of Greek Workmanship.* 3 vols. Naples, 1791–1795, Tischbein.

Hannover, Emil. "Europe and Near East; Earthenware and Stoneware," *Pottery and Porcelain,* I, tr. by B. Rackham. London, 1925, Ernest Baur.

Hautecoeur, Louis. *Rome et la Renaissance de d'Antiquité à la Fin du XVIIIe Siècle,* Fascicule 105, Bibliothèque des Ecoles Francaises d'Athènes et de Rome. Paris, 1912, Fontemoing.

Helbig, Wolfgang. *Wandgemälde der vom Vesuv Verschütteten Städte Campaniens.* Leipzig, 1868, Breitkopf and Härtel.

Hinks, R. P. *Catalogue of the Greek, Etruscan, and Roman Painting and Mosaics in the British Museum.* 1933.

Hobson, Robert Lockhart. *Catalogue of English Pottery in the British Museum.* London, 1903.

Hoppin, Joseph C. *A Handbook of Attic Red-figured Vases . . .* 2 Vols. Cambridge [Mass.], 1919, Harvard University Press.

Illustrated Catalogue of Beautiful Old Wedgwood . . . Belonging to Horace Townsend. New York, 1914, American Art Association.

Jewitt, Llewellyn. *The History of Ceramic Art in Great Britain.* 2 vols. New York, 1878, Scribner.

――――. *The Wedgwoods: Being a Life of Josiah Wedgwood.* London, 1865, Virtue Brothers.

Jones, H. Stuart, "British School at Rome: Miscellanea Capitolina," *Athenaeum,* February 27, 1909.

――――, ed. *Catalogue of the Ancient Sculptures . . . of the Museo Capitolino,* British School at Rome. Oxford, 1912, Clarendon Press.

――――, ed. *A Catalogue of the Ancient Sculptures . . . of the Palazzo dei Conservatori,* British School at Rome. Oxford, 1926, Clarendon Press.

Kimball, Fiske. "Romantic Classicism in Architecture," *Gazette des Beaux-Arts,* XXVI, 6th series, February, 1944, pp. 95–112.

King, Charles W. *Antique Gems and Rings.* 2 vols. London, 1872, Bell and Daldy.

――――. *Handbook of Engraved Gems.* London, 1866, Bell and Daldy.

Kris, Ernst. *Meister und Meisterwerke der Steinschneiderkunst in der Italienischen Renaissance,* Vienna, 1929, Schroll.

La Chausse, Michel-ange de. *Le Gemme Antiche Figurate.* Rome and Parigino, 1720.

Lippold, Georg. *Gemmen und Kameen des Altertums und der Neuzeit.* Stuttgart, n.d., Julius Hoffman.

――――. *Die Skulpturen des Vaticanischen Museums.* Berlin and Leipzig, 1936.

Maclagan, Eric, and Margaret H. Longhurst. *Catalogue of Italian Sculpture in the Victoria and Albert Museum.* London, 1932.

Maffei, Paolo Alessandro, and Domenico de Rossi. *Gemme Antiche Figurate.* 4 vols. Rome, 1708.

――――. *Raccolta di Statue Antiche e Moderne.* Rome, 1704.

Manners, Lady Victoria and Dr. C. Williamson, *Angelica Kauffmann,* n.d., New York, Brentano.

Marconi, Pirro. *La Pittura dei Romani.* Rome, 1929, Biblioteca d'Arte.

Mariette, P. J. *Traité des Pierres Gravées et un Recueil des Pierres Gravées du Cabinet du Roy.* 2 vols. Paris, 1750, Mariette.

Méautis, Georges. *Chefs d'Oeuvre de la Peinture Grecque.* Paris, 1939, Albin Michel.

Meteyard, Eliza. *Choice Examples of Wedgwood Art.* London, 1879, George Bell.

————. *The Life of Josiah Wedgwood from his Private Correspondence and Family Papers with an Introductory Sketch of the Art of Pottery in England.* 2 vols. London, 1866, Hurst and Blackett.

————. *Memorials of Wedgwood.* London, 1874, George Bell.

————. *Wedgwood and His Works.* London, 1873, Bell and Daldy.

————. *The Wedgwood Handbook.* London, 1875, George Bell.

Michaelis, Adolph. *Ancient Marbles in Great Britain.* Cambridge, 1882.

————. "Das Grabmal der Nasonier," *Jahrbuch des Kaiserlich Deutschen Archäologischen Instituts,* XXV, 1910, pp. 101 ff.

————. *Der Parthenon.* Leipzig, 1871, Breitkopf and Härtel.

Middleton, J. Henry. *The Engraved Gems of Classical Times with a Catalogue of the Gems in the Fitzwilliam Museum.* Cambridge, 1891, University Press.

Montfaucon, Bernard de. *Antiquité Expliquée.* 5 vols., supplement 5 vols. Paris, 1719.

Moore, N. Hudson. *Wedgwood and His Imitators.* New York, 1909, Frederick A. Stokes.

Müller, C. O. *Ancient Art and Its Remains,* new ed. by F. G. Welcker, tr. by John Leitch. London, 1852, Bernard Quaritch.

Murray, A. S. *Handbook of Greek Archaeology.* New York, 1892, Scribner.

Museum Worsleyanum; or A Collection of Antique Bassi-relievos, Bustos, Statues and Gems. 2 vols. London, 1824, Septimuse Prowett.

Musée National du Louvre, Catalogue Sommaire des Marbres Antiques. Paris, 1922.

Natter, Laurentius. *A Treatise on the Ancient Method of Engraving on Precious Stones.* London, 1754.

Ogle, George. *Antiquities Explained; being a Collection of Figured Gems.* London, 1737, James Bettenham.

Old Wedgwood; the Frank Gunsaulus Collection Acquired from the Collection of Arthur Sanderson. Chicago, Art Institute, 1916.

Osborne, S. Duffield. *Engraved Gems.* New York, 1912, Henry Holt.

Passeri, J. B. *Picturae Etruscorum.* 3 vols. Rome, 1747, Hohannis Zempel.

Perrier, François. *Segmanta Nobilium Signorum e Statuarii.* Rome, 1638.

Picart, Bernard. *Tempel der Zang-Godinnen.* Amsterdam, 1733, Zacharias Chatelain.

Piroli, Tommaso. *Le Antichitá di Ercolano,* 6 vols. in 3, Rome, 1789.

Piroli, Tommaso, and Giorgio Zoega. *Li Bassirilievi Antichi di Roma.* Rome, 1808, Francesco Bourlié.

Pistolesi, Erasmo. *Antiquities of Herculaneum and Pompeii.* Naples, 1842, Royal Press.

————. *Reale Museo Borbonico.* Rome, 1840, Gismondi.

————. *Il Vaticano.* 8 vols. Rome, 1829.

Praz, Mario. "Herculaneum and European Taste," *Magazine of Art,* XXXII, 1939, p. 686 ff.

Prime, William C. *Pottery and Porcelain of All Times and Nations.* New York, 1878, Harper.

Rackham, Bernard. *Catalogue of the Herbert Allen Collection of English Porcelain in the Victoria and Albert Museum.* 2nd ed. London, 1923.

Rackham, Bernard, and Herbert Read. *English Pottery.* London, 1924, E. Benn.

Raoul-Rochette, Desirée. *Monumens Inédits d'Antiquité Grecque, Etrusque, et Romaine.* Paris, 1826–1833.

Raspe, R. E. *Catalogue Raisonné d'une Collection Genérale de Pierres Gravées Antiques et Modernes . . .* London, 1791, J. Murray.

Rathbone, Frederick. *A Catalogue of the Wedgwood Museum, Etruria.* Stoke-on-Trent, 1909, J. Wedgwood.

———. *Old Wedgwood.* London, 1898, Bernard Quaritch.

Reinach, Salomon. *Peintures de Vases Antiques.* Paris, 1891, Firmin-Didot.

———. *Pierres Gravées.* Paris, 1895, Firmin-Didot.

———. *Répertoire de la Statuaire Grecque et Romaine.* 6 vols. Paris, 1897, Ernest Leroux.

———. *Répertoire de Peintures Grecques et Romaines.* Paris, 1922, Leroux.

———. *Répertoire de Reliefs Grecs et Romains.* 3 vols. Paris, 1912.

———. *Répertoire des Vases Peints.* 2 vols. 2nd ed. Paris, 1922, Ernest Leroux.

Rhead, G. Woolliscroft, and Frederick Allen Rhead. *Staffordshire Pots and Potters.* London, 1906, Hutchinson.

Richter, Gisela M. A. *Catalogue of Engraved Gems of the Classical Style in the Metropolitan Museum of Art.* New York, 1920.

———. *The Sculpture and Sculptors of the Greeks.* New Haven, 1930, Yale University Press.

Riegl, Alois. *Spätrömische Kunstindustrie.* Vienna, 1927.

Righetti, Pietro. *Descrizione del Campidoglio.* 2 vols. Rome, 1835.

Rizzo, G. E. *La Pittura Ellenistico-Romana.* Milan, 1929, Fratelli Treres.

Robert, Carl. *Die Antiken Sarkophag-Reliefs.* Vol. II, 1890, Vol. III, 1897. Berlin.

Roscher, W. H. *Ausführliches Lexikon der Griechischen und Römischen Mythologie.* Leipzig, 1894–1897, Teubner.

Roux, H., and M. L. Barré. *Herculaneum et Pompeii.* 8 vols. Paris, Firmin-Didot, 1820.

Sandys, Sir John Edwin. *A History of Classical Scholarship.* 3 vols. Cambridge, 1908.

Sculture della Villa Borghese. 2 vols. Rome, 1796, Pagliannini.

Shaw, Simeon. *History of the Staffordshire Potteries.* Hanley, 1829.

Smith, Cecil H. *Vases of the Finest Period. Catalogue of the Greek and Etruscan Vases in the British Museum,* III. London, 1896.

Solon, Louis Marc Emmanuel. *Ceramic Literature; An Analytical Index.* London, 1910, Chas. Griffin and Company.

Spence, Joseph. *Polymetis.* London, Tully's Head, Pall-Mall, 1747.

Spinozzola, Vittorio. *Le Arti Decorative in Pompeii e nel Museo Nazionale di Napoli*. Milan, 1928.

Stosch, Philippe de. *Pierres Antiques Gravées*. Amsterdam, 1727, Bernard Picart.

Strong, Eugenie. *Roman Sculpture*. London, 1907, Duckworth.

Stuart, James, and Nicholas Revett. *Die Alterthümer zu Athen*. Leipzig and Darmstadt, n.d., C. W. Leke.

Swarbrick, John. *Robert Adam and His Brothers*. London, 1915, Batsford.

Swindler, Mary Hamilton. *Ancient Painting*. New Haven, 1929, Yale University Press.

Tassie, James. *Catalogue of Impressions in Sulphur of Antique and Modern Gems*. London, 1775, Murray.

Toynbee, Jocelyn. *The Hadrianic School*. Cambridge, 1934, University Press.

Turnbull, George. *A Treatise on Ancient Painting*. London, 1740, A. Miller.

Visconti, E. Q., and le Comte de Clarac. *Description des Antiques du Musée Royale*. Paris, 1820, Mme. Hérissant Le Doux.

Wace, Alan John B. "The Reliefs in the Palazzo Spada," *Papers of the British School at Rome*, V, pp. 83 ff. London, 1910.

Waldstein, Charles, and Leonard Shoobridge. *Herculaneum: Past, Present, and Future*. London, 1908, Macmillan.

Walters, Henry Beauchamp. *Catalogue of Engraved Gems and Cameos in the British Museum*. London, 1926.

———. *Catalogue of the Terracottas in the Department of Greek and Roman Antiquities in the British Museum*. London, 1903.

———. *Vases of the Latest Period. Catalogue of the Greek and Etruscan Vases in the British Museum*, IV. London, 1896.

Wedgwood, Josiah, *Letters, 1762–1794*, 3 vols. London, 1903, privately printed.

Wedgwood, Josiah Clement. *History of the Wedgwood Family*. London, 1908, St. Catherine Press.

———. *Staffordshire Pottery and Its History*. London, 1913, S. Low, Marstor and Company.

Wicar and Mongez. *Galérie de Florence; Tableaux, Statues, Bas-reliefs et Camées*. Paris, 1804.

Williamson, George. *The Imperial Russian Dinner Service*. London, 1909, George Bell.

Winckelmann, Johann Joachim. *Description des Pierres Gravées du feu Baron de Stosch*. Florence, 1760, Andre Bonducci.

———. *Monumenti Antichi Inediti*. 2 vols. Rome, 1767.

Worlidge, T. *A Select Collection of Drawings from Curious Antique Gems*. London, 1768, Dryden Leach.

Index
